PUBLIC SPEAKING
PLUS

COMMUNICATION SKILLS FOR CAREER SUCCESS

Thomas J. Farrell
Associate Professor, Chairman-Humanities Department
Johnson & Wales College

with

Robert E. Burns, M.A.
Assistant Professor
Johnson & Wales College

P.A.R. Incorporated
Abbott Park Place, Providence, Rhode Island

Public Speaking Plus
Communication Skills for Career Success
Copyright © 1984 by P.A.R. Incorporated

Printed in the United States of America
ISBN 0-89702-044-8

TABLE OF CONTENTS

Preface

PART ONE: INTRAPERSONAL COMMUNICATION

Chapter 1

PART TWO: INTERPERSONAL COMMUNICATION

Chapter 2

Chapter 3

Chapter 4

PART THREE: PUBLIC SPEAKING FOR BUSINESS

Chapter 5

Chapter 6

Chapter 7

Chapter 8

PART FOUR: OTHER COMMUNICATION SKILLS FOR CAREER SUCCESS

Chapter 9

Chapter 10

Chapter 11

Chapter 12

Chapter 13

PART FIVE: WRITTEN COMMUNICATION FOR BUSINESS

Chapter 14

Chapter 15

Preface

Public Speaking Plus is a book that students will want to keep long beyond graduation. They will return to it often as they pursue their goals in life. In it, students will find the keys to success in their business careers as well as their interpersonal relationships.

The fundamental premise on which the book is built is that to be a success, one must communicate effectively. This innovative text was designed to be used in a *Public Speaking* course as well as to serve as a guide through the full range of other communication skills. It is this multi-dimensional appeal which we feel is a *plus* for students. Special attention is made to show the students how each communication skill may be used in business situations.

The book is organized into five major parts. The first, **INTRAPERSONAL COMMUNICATION,** explains the relationship between success and effective communication skills and asks the students to evaluate their own strengths and weaknesses as communicators. The basic premise here is that an honest self-inventory is necessary before any change can take place.

The second part, **INTERPERSONAL COMMUNICATION,** returns to basics and reminds students of fundamental communication principles. Special sections are devoted to listening and non-verbal communication.

The third and major section of the book, **PUBLIC SPEAKING FOR BUSINESS,** covers the traditional theories of speech making. Recognizing that fear of public speaking is the *# 1 phobia* in our society, material on how to deal with speech anxiety starts the section. Methods of preparing and delivering speeches are presented along with discussions of different types of speeches. Models and critique sheets are provided at the end of the section.

The fourth part, **OTHER COMMUNICATION SKILLS FOR CAREER SUCCESS,** addresses a variety of skills that students must learn to master; often, those skills are not dealt with in college communications courses. Lively and informative treatments of interviewing, corporate life, the language used in business, small group problem-solving and telephone techniques are included.

Finally, to insure that students are fully equipped with all of the necessary communication skills for success, the fifth part, **WRITTEN COMMUNICATION FOR BUSINESS,** covers current approaches to written business correspondence, including explanations of the style and format for memos, business letters, and reports. Some material in this section is exerpted from my book *Developing Writing Skills* and is included for the use of faculty who choose to include correspondence in their communications courses and for the practical benefit of students who will need to write well in their work.

Public Speaking Plus is a book that will have positive effects on students' lives and careers. That is what it is designed to do and that is the hope.

I would like to thank my associate, Robert Burns, for the assistance he provided researching material for this book. Also, my thanks to Deborah King and Joanne Galenski for their help preparing the manuscript.

Thomas J. Farrell

Intrapersonal
Communication

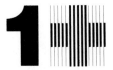

SUCCESS AND EFFECTIVE COMMUNICATION SKILLS

Every four years athletes from all over the world gather together to compete in the Olympic games. The athletes' goals are to represent their countries to the best of their abilities and, if they are the best, to take home the coveted gold medal. In 1984, the competitors met at Sarajevo, Yugoslavia, and Los Angeles, California; practice has already begun for the 1988 games. Young men and women are working hard to perfect their specialty, whether it be in swimming, basketball, distance running, skating, or some other sport. Each has the same objective: *to succeed, to win the gold*.

As college students, you are very much like those Olympic athletes. You too train for two or four years with a clear objective in mind. You too look forward to the day when you can represent your family and your school with pride in the competitive world of business. Even your goal is similar to the Olympic athlete: *to succeed, to do the best work of which you are capable*. All your college courses are geared toward helping you achieve your goal, but the course (or courses) that will help you the most is the course that focuses on improving your communication skills. It may be called Public Speaking, Speech, Communication Skills, or something else in your curriculum. The course title is not so important, but the course content is vital. Make it your specialty.

You might think of this book as a training manual that provides a program which, if followed, will prepare you to be a winner in the competitive world that waits for you after graduation. Work on each part of the program as your instructor suggests in the same way you would respond to the directions of a coach. Be enthusiastic; enjoy what you are doing and take pride in your growth and development. Be confident that, with sincere effort on your part, you too can be a winner. *You can be successful!*

Communication Skills in an Informational Society

It is *essential* that you understand and accept the premise that the most important factor in determining your future success is how well you communicate with others. Believe it; for it is fact. Should you need more convincing, consider the following statements:

- The Midwest College Placement Association conducted a study aimed at learning what skills and qualities employers look for in hiring. The results were revealing. The first choice was oral communication skills (83% ranked it as very important), and the third choice was interpersonal skills (74% ranked it as very important).[1]

- The prestigious *Harvard Business Review* is very direct in its viewpoint, "The prime requisite for success and promotion in business is the ability to communicate."[2]

- In the Preface to *Effective Communication on the Job,* the editor, William K. Fallon, is equally emphatic. "Good communication skills are surely among the most important ingredients of business success. Even if you aren't a salesperson, you have a selling job to do throughout your entire career. You have a product to sell — and that product is you! Whatever your job is, you must get messages across to people, whether they are your subordinates, your peers, or your bosses."[3]

- Finally, Nancy L. Harper and John Waite Bowers writing in *Communication and Your Career* echo the others, "Even if communication skills are applicable only to selected portions of your future jobs, however, chances are you won't be successful if you cannot communicate."[4]

Convinced? If so, then the conclusion is inescapable. To be successful, you must strive to be an effective communicator.

To some degree, this has always been the case but, today, more than ever, it is a basic requirement in business. The reason for this is, that along with everything else in our lives, the nature of work in our country has changed. In the recent bestseller, *Megatrends,* John Naisbitt sketched a brief occupational history of the United States which is helpful to an understanding of our point.

Until 1956, we lived and worked in what was called an "industrial society," so called because most people were blue-collar workers working at jobs where they produced goods. In 1956, for the first time, white-collar workers outnumbered blue-collar workers. Industrial America was giving way to a new society where most of us worked with information rather than producing goods.[5]

Today, the industrial and post-industrial societies are gone and, in their place, the informational society has arrived, a society in which the need to communicate well is more critical that it ever was. The largest job classification in our economy is clerk and the second largest is professional. More than 65% of Americans work with information as programmers, teachers, clerks, secretaries, accountants, stockbrokers, managers, insurance agents, bureaucrats, lawyers, bankers, and technicians.[6] Your chance of being employed in the information sector of our economy is far greater than your being employed in the fading industrial sector.

At the same time the informational society was evolving, other social and cultural changes were occurring.

The work place has become more humanized with better-educated workers insisting that their work be more personally satisfying and that they be treated as individual people rather than as cogs in a machine. The drill sergeant model of management has passed away — even in the Army. Cooperation, *communication,* and conciliation are the order of the day in business.[7] In this fresh and exciting environment, people who possess a wide range of communication skills are not only sought after by employers but valued as key employees.

How to Make It Happen

The two keys to improving your communication skills are *awareness* and *change.* To start, you must evaluate your own strengths and weaknesses as communicators. What are you presently doing well? What not so well? What do you understand about your own personality and how it relates to communication? Are you knowledgeable about current theories of communication that are the result of recent research? Once this honest inventory has been taken, you are ready to begin behavioral change to improve your skills. Like the Olympic athlete in training, you can set your goals and begin working to achieve them.

PERSONALITY AND COMMUNICATION

Your effort to develop communication skills that will contribute to a successful career must start with self-evaluation.
Before you go forward, you must look backward. You have
already lived a significant span of your life and, in the process,
formed a personality which directly influences the way you
interact with others. It is necessary that you reflect for a while
on just how you became the person you are and why each of
you has a personality distinct from one another.

Social scientists define *personality* as a system of beliefs,
attitudes, and behaviors which are the particular qualities and
characteristics of a person.

There are many theories explaining how personalities develop, but it is not our purpose to present detailed explanations
of these theories. That is more the function of a psychology or
sociology textbook. However, we can generalize by noting
that these theories take one of two broad approaches: biological
determinism or cultural determinism. Simply stated, biologi-
cally deterministic theories suggest that genetic factors have a
greater impact on human behavior than was previously
thought. Culturally deterministic theories claim that environment, the things we are exposed to in our lives, is the primary
influence that molds our personalities. The truth probably lies
somewhere between the two theories and there is still much
that we have to learn. We can, however, acknowledge the
biological theories and still claim that our personalities are
primarily the result of the cultural stimuli we receive during the
socialization process.

If your personality is the product of socialization, you need
to know more about that process. Socialization is the way that
you acquire your human personality: that is, the process in
which you learn the skills, values, attitudes, and role behaviors
that you use in life. For most of you, the most important
influences during your socialization were your parents, the
teachers in the schools you attended, your religious education,
the friends you have, and, today more than ever before, television and other media that help shape your views. It might be
useful at this point for you to try to connect some of your
positive personality characteristics with the socializing factor
you consider most responsible for each characteristic. Choose
any ten of your personal qualities that you consider to be positive and write them in the spaces provided. Next to the ones

that you choose, indicate whether your parents, your teachers, your religion, your peers, or television and other media have been the major factors shaping that part of your personality.

Exercise I

Positive Quality or Characteristic	*Major Influence*
example: competitive	father
1. *responsible*	*mother*
2. *competitive*	*friends*
3. *conservative*	
4. *caring*	*mother*
5. *somewhat religious*	*school/grand-parent*
6. *attractive*	*mom/dad*
7. *hard worker*	*family*
8.	
9.	
10.	

When you have completed the exercise, take a few moments to think about the choices you have made. What do they tell you about your personality and how it has been formed? Clearly, your selections say a lot about your self-image which is so vital to developing effective communication skills. You have a positive self-image when you see and evaluate yourself in terms that are consistent with the person you ideally want to be. When this occurs, you are able to present yourself to others in a manner that will lead to successful and productive communication.

The reverse is also true. Negative self-images (which may also result from the socialization process) make effective communication difficult, if not impossible. Since very few people have entirely positive (or negative) self-images, you need to identify those personality traits which are not consistent with the person you really wish to be. As before, see if you can connect each undesirable trait you write down with the major socializing influence responsible for it. For example, if you started smoking as a teenager because of peer pressure (as many teenagers do), you would list smoking as a negative personality characteristic with "friends" as the major influence.

Exercise II

	Negative Quality or Characteristic	*Major Influence*
1.	procrastinator	family / friend
2.	drink/alcohol	family
3.	cus too much	friends
4.	overweight	mom
5.	low self image	friends
6.		
7.		
8.		
9.		
10.		

Once again, think about the choices you have written down and the connections you made. What else do they tell you about your personality and how it was formed? Which of the two lists was easier to complete? How do you feel about your self-image? Positively? Negatively? Mixed? ... Whatever the results of this initial self-evaluation, remember that your personality is the product of your socialization. It is important that you keep that in mind as we consider some new knowledge about the socialization process.

SOCIALIZATION IS ONGOING — CHANGE IS POSSIBLE

It wasn't too long ago that the common belief was that our personality was fully formed by the time we finished adolescence and little fundamental change occurred after that point in our lives. That idea has now been set aside. While it is still recognized that the most significant socialization occurs during childhood and adolescence, there is now widespread agreement that change and development continue on an ongoing basis into old age. Erik Erikson and Orville G. Brim, Jr. are two theorists who contend that substantial personality change and development do occur throughout our lifetimes.

Erikson's *Eight Stages of Human Development* (See box — pp. 8-10) suggest that, as we move through the stages of our lives, we encounter difficult challenges that need to be met and dealt with before we are able to go on to the next stage. An award-winning 1983 movie, *Terms of Endearment,* illustrates this point well. In it Shirley McLaine plays a fiftyish widow who has cut herself off from relationships with men. Jack Nicholson plays a middle-aged ex-astronaut who lives a dissipated life, capitalizing on past glories. At the movie's end, after the tragic death of a daughter, the two are changed people who come together in a loving relationship. As a means of helping you continue to evaluate your personality, read the description of each of Erikson's stages to see the challenges you have already met and ones you have yet to face. Keep in mind: *change is possible.*

Brim's theory stresses the differences between childhood socialization and the socialization of adults. Two of his points are of special importance to you as you prepare to learn the communication skills that are necessary to career success:

- Adult socialization is more likely to change overt behavior, whereas childhood socialization molds basic values.

- Adult socialization is designed to help a person gain specific skills; childhood socialization deals more with motivation.[8]

The course you are taking and this textbook you are reading are both part of *your* ongoing adult socialization process. If Brim is correct, and there is general support for his views, feel confident that you can change your present communication habits and acquire the skills that you need to accomplish your goals.

**Habits: Break
Bad Ones —
Learn New
Ones**

Before you begin to consider this program of self-improve-ment, another insight into your personality may be helpful. Do you know that to a large extent, our everyday behaviors are patterned, and quite predictable. This is so because we are creatures of habit who tend to repeat and reinforce our be-haviors until they become automatic. According to William Brown, chairman of the Sociology Department at the Univer-sity of Florida, 90 percent of our behavior could be called habitual.[9] This reliance on habit helps us cope with our every-day lives and makes life easier. Think of all the behaviors you engage in each day by habit, without thinking out each detail of what you are doing. When you drive a car or play a sport, you are acting by habit. This is all for the good.

Unfortunately, habitual behavior has its negative side. We can just as easily learn incorrect, non-productive habits as we can correct, productive ones, and we do. For example, if you are like most people, you probably are not a good listener which means you have acquired ineffective listening habits (see Part III — Listening). *All habits are difficult to break* but they can be broken and replaced with different and stronger habits. To do this you need the desire, the will, and the knowl-edge. That is, you have to want to change, be willing to work hard at doing so, and have access to the information necessary for change. If you have these three requirements, you can begin to identify the person you really are, develop a positive self-image, and learn how to communicate with others in ways that will lead to success.

**ERIKSON'S EIGHT STAGES
OF
HUMAN DEVELOPMENT**

1. TRUST vs. MISTRUST *(infancy)*
From nursing, diaper changing, napping and cud-dling, babies learn to what extent their basic needs will be met. When infants are secure enough so that they no longer feel rage or anger when their caregiver goes away, the first crisis in development has been resolved. Traces of mistrust may remain, however, resolution often is not complete.

---

2. *AUTONOMY vs. SHAME AND DOUBT* *(1-2 yrs.)*

The child learns how to talk, learns to run without falling down, and acquires much more knowledge about the world. This is when self-assertion and defiance of authority blossom. At the same time, it is the stage in which parents usually attempt bowel training. Too many demands in this area can instill a strong sense of shame and worthlessness in the child and undermine his or her efforts to achieve autonomy and self-direction.

3. *INITIATIVE vs. GUILT* *(3-5 yrs.)*

This period is one of movement, curiosity, and imagination. Rivalry and awareness of sex differences are prominent at this stage. As a result, the child experiences conflict over how far to take the initiative in asserting new abilities.

4. *INDUSTRY vs. INFERIORITY* *(early school yrs.)*

Children learn to carry out individual tasks like reading books and collective tasks like classroom work projects. They form relationships with teachers and other adults. They become interested in real-life roles: fire-fighter, pilot, nurse. Their most important task, however, is to gain self-confidence and competence, since it is during this stage that children are introduced to (and act out in their fantasies) actual adult roles. Unsuccessful resolution of this crisis leaves a child feeling inferior and inadequate.

5. *IDENTITY vs. ROLE DIFFUSION* *(adolescence)*

Two major events occur at this time. Physically, young people become adults with an active sex drive; they are also expected to find a niche in society. The adolescent must decide whether to go to college, find a job, and choose a mate. Failure to do so may disrupt later attempts to choose suitable jobs, partners, and friends.

6. *INTIMACY vs. ISOLATION* *(early adulthood)*
Courtship, marriage, and other types of intimacy are the key objectives during this stage. The person seeks an open, trusting relationship, usually with a permanent mate; this may, however, fail and lead to separation or divorce. If the conflict between intimacy and isolation is not resolved, the person may go through a series of temporary, always-broken relationships.

7. *GENERATIVITY vs. STAGNATION*
(middle adulthood)
This stage is concerned mainly with coming to terms with work and parenting. How ambitious is the person? How early does he or she burn out in a work career? Can he or she successfully generate new members of society through birth and caring? How are failures in work and parenting coped with?

8. *INTEGRITY vs. DESPAIR* *(late adulthood)*
In this phase the person sums up his or her life, grows old gracefully or bitterly, and perhaps takes on some new philosophical view of life. If the person is satisfied with his or her life, the result is a sense of integrity. If not, the outcome is despair.[10]

THREE TYPES OF COMMUNICATORS

Another method of identifying the person you really are is to try to place yourself in one of the broad categories of communications types characterized below: the Cooperative Communicator, the Dominating Communicator, and the Yielding Communicator. While it is true that your behavior as communicators will vary depending on the people you are with and the situation you are in, it is probably equally true that certain patterns or habits tend to characterize our behavior *most* of the time. Whatever your own repetitive patterns are will determine which category you belong to; write "yes" after the characteristic that describes your communications behavior *most* of the time and "no" where the characteristic occurs infrequently or not at all. The category with the most "yeses" may in fact be the one to which you presently belong.

The Cooperative Communicator

- Encourages dialogue and is willing to listen to another person's point of view.

- Works for joint understanding and solutions to problems so that goals may be attained.

- Offers new ideas and suggestions willingly.

- Recognizes that he/she is not always right and that to be wrong is, indeed, quite human.

- Looks for new ways of doing things and is not reluctant to "stick one's neck out" by experimentation.

The Dominating Communicator

- Is strictly a one-way communicator.

- Feels that his/her own ideas are best and does not listen to others.

- Imposes his/her own point of view on others whenever possible.

- Is not open to alternative approaches to accomplishing objectives.

- Tries to preserve the status quo and does not encourage experimentation.

The Yielding Communicator

- Is passive and shifts the responsibility for communication to the other person.

- Believes that other people have more to contribute than he/she does. (Often, it becomes clear, after the fact, that this is not the case.)

- Allows himself/herself to be manipulated by other people even when he/she knows what is happening.

- Assumes that nothing can be done to improve a situation so why bother trying.

- Will consider alternatives and experiments only if others are responsible for the outcome.

Once you have studied the three types of communicators, which of the three do you feel describes you best? Obviously, in today's "informational" society, the more "cooperative" characteristics you possess the better prepared you will be to participate in the new wave that is sweeping management-employee relations in our economy. The "dominating" communicators are still to be found but, like the dinosaurs of the Mesozoic Era, they are a vanishing breed who will soon be extinct. Finally, it is self evident that the "yielding" communicator is one who is not going to share in the potential rewards of a successful business career. As was discussed earlier, change is possible. *Work to become a "cooperative" communicator.*

YOUR COMMUNICATIONS QUOTIENT —
A PERSONAL ASSESSMENT

In order for you to further inventory your communications skills, take a few minutes to do this personal assessment test. This is a general test that will give you some understanding of your pluses and minuses as a communicator. The test should also be a starting point for you to evaluate your "communications quotient" or your communications awareness. Please keep in mind that there are no right or wrong answers. Simply answer the questions honestly. Usually the first answer that comes to mind is your best answer. The questions that follow explore various areas of communication that we will discuss throughout the book. These questions cover the following areas: listening, nonverbal communication, public speaking and presentational skills, speech anxiety, intrapersonal communication, interviewing, small group communication, and interpersonal communication.

Please answer the questions as follows:

1/ Always   2/ Sometimes   3/ Never

If you are asked the following question: "I enjoy speaking before audiences.", write the number that best fits your position. If you don't enjoy it, you would write #3. Or if the question reads: "My friends seek me out because they know I listen well." Write #2 if you believe you "sometimes" listen well.

Work carefully and alone on the questions. Do not consult with your classmates.
Please write your answer in the space provided. Write 1, 2, or 3 only.

1. ___2___ I know the right thing to say in all types of environments.

2. ___2___ I look forward to speaking before all types of audiences.

3. ___2___ I am sought out to represent others when they can't represent themselves.

4. ___2___ People recognize me as a good listener.

5. ___2___ I withhold evaluation while I am listening until I have heard all the facts.

6. ___2___ I can accept compliments without embarrassment.

7. ___2___ I try to write all the facts down when I'm listening to a lecturer.

8. ___2___ My emotions do not interfere with my ability to listen.

9. ___3___ I enjoy debating all types of topics.

10. ___3___ I look forward to the challenges of taking an interview for a job.

11. ___2___ I enjoy interviewing people to work for me.

12. ___2___ I find myself reacting to ideas instead of the personality of the speaker.

13. ___2___ People compliment me on my smile.

14. ___2___ It is easy for me to concentrate and get rid of distractions when I am working.

15. ___3___ Speaking in public is something I relish.

16. ___2___ I know what is required of me in all communicative settings.

17. ___3___ I am looked upon as an extrovert.

18. ___1___ One of my communications strengths is my voice.

19. ___1___ I am considered a person who knows how to dress for the occasion.

20. ___3___ When participating in small groups, I like to take a primary role in directing the other group members.

21. ___3___ When meeting people for the first time, I never find myself at a loss for words.

22. ___2___ Discussing controversial topics is something I handle well.

23. ___3___ When speaking with others, one on one, I find myself reinforcing my messages by the use of examples and illustrations.

24. ___3___ When speaking with others, I maintain eye contact.

25. ___3___ I like to voice my opinions in groups.

26. ___3___ I look forward to breaking down in small groups to discuss the resolutions of problems.

27. ___2___ I know how to get people to do things for me with little difficulty.

28. ___1___ Getting along with others is easy for me.

29. ___2___ I would be a good salesperson because I'm a persuasive speaker.

30. ___2___ I am aware of the nonverbal messages others transmit.

31. ___2___ I like to give directions to others.

32. ___2___ People look upon me as a good judge of character.

33. ___3___ I have a strong self-image.

34. ___3___ I am relaxed when in a room full of strangers.

35. ___2___ One of the things people compliment me on is my good attitude.

36. ___2___ I understand social custom and the rules of etiquette.

37. ___3___ When I come right down to it, I consider myself a superior communicator.

38. ___2___ I find it easy to control my temper and emotions.

39. ___2___ I consider speaking before others a privilege and an important opportunity.

40. ___2___ I listen to others without daydreaming.

41. ___2___ I speak positively to myself as part of a "stage-fright" reduction technique.

42. ___2___ When a person smiles at me, I know it could mean many different things. Therefore, I don't jump to conclusions when interpreting messages.

43. ___1___ I am looked upon as an understanding and sympathetic friend.

44. ___2___ Before speaking, regardless of the environment, I do my research.

45. ___2___ A sales presentation is an exciting opportunity for me.

46. ___2___ When interacting with others interpersonally or one on one, I am successful.

47. ___2___ When I am involved with clubs or organizations I like to function in a leadership role.

48. ___2___ I understand the interviewing process and feel confident that I could successfully answer the questions an interviewer is likely to ask.

49. ___3___ When it comes to controversy or settling disputes, people seek me out as a claiming influence.

50. ___3___ Shyness is never a barrier to my interaction.

Remember, there are no right or wrong answers.

Next, write the number of the questions that you answered 3, 2, or 1, and fill in below; refer to the next page for additional directions.

1 - ALWAYS		2 - SOMETIMES		3 - NEVER	
Ques. No.	Skill	Ques. No.	Skill	Ques. No.	Skill
18	Intra-Personal	4		1	
19	Intra-Personal	5		2	
28	Inter-Personal	6		3	
43	Intra-Personal	7		9	
		8		10	
		11		15	
		12		17	
		13		20	
		14		21	
		16		23	
		22		24	
		27		25	
		29		26	
		30		33	
		31		34	
		32		37	
		35		49	
		36	44-48	50	
		38			
		39			
		40			
		41			

Ques. No.	Skill	Ques. No.	Skill	Ques. No.	Skill

Now, from the chart below, fill in next to the question number the kind of skill involved in each question. The ones that crop up most frequently in column 3 are the areas in which you need the most help; column 2 suggests areas where your self-evaluation is mixed; column 1 should be your strengths.

1. Public speaking - presentational
2. Public speaking
3. Interpersonal
4. Listening
5. Listening
6. Interpersonal
7. Listening
8. Listening
9. Small Groups
10. Interviewing
11. Interviewing
12. Listening
13. Interpersonal
14. Interpersonal
15. Public Speaking
16. General
17. Intrapersonal
18. Intrapersonal
19. Intrapersonal
20. Small Groups
21. Interpersonal
22. Interpersonal
23. Interpersonal
24. Nonverbal
25. Small Groups
26. Small Groups
27. Interpersonal
28. Interpersonal
29. Interpersonal
30. Nonverbal
31. Interpersonal
32. Intrapersonal
33. Intrapersonal
34. Interpersonal
35. Intrapersonal
36. Interpersonal
37. Intrapersonal
38. Intrapersonal
39. Public Speaking
40. Listening
41. Speech Anxiety
42. Nonverbal
43. Intrapersonal
44. Public Speaking
45. Presentational
46. Interpersonal
47. Small Groups
48. Interviewing
49. Interpersonal
50. Intrapersonal

Endnotes

1 *Principles of Speech Communication* by Douglas Ehninger, Bruce E. Gronbeck, and Alan H. Munroe.

2 *Harvard Business Review.*

3 *Effective Communication on the Job* by William K. Fallon.

4 "Communication in Your Career" by Nancy L. Harper and John Waite Bowers.

5 *Megatrends* by John Naisbitt.

6 *Megatrends* by John Naisbitt.

7 "You're OK, Boss!" by Terry Porro in *Notre Dame Magazine*.

8 *Sociology* by Neil Smelser.

9 "Those Great Decisions of Yours May Be Just Habits" by Jeff Kunerth in the *Orlando Central*.

10 *Sociology* by Neil Smelser.

Interpersonal Communication

2

INTERPERSONAL COMMUNICATION

Up to this point, the discussion in this text has focused on two major parts: 1/ the need to become an effective communicator if you are to succeed in an informational society, 2/ the necessity of assessing your own personality and understanding how it reflects in strengths and/or weaknesses as a communicator. Further, you learned that *change is possible;* negative habits that will get in the way of career success can be exchanged for positive ones.

If you have accepted the two major concepts summarized above, you are now ready to switch from an introspective look at yourself to the actual process of becoming a more skilled interpersonal communicator. Earlier, we indicated that the two keys necessary to improving communication skills were *Awareness* and *Change*. In his book, *Reaching Out,* David W. Johnson is more specific when he outlines the first three steps needed to learn new interpersonal skills:

1/ Becoming aware of the need for and uses of a new skill.

2/ Identifying the behaviors involved in the new skill.

3/ Using the behaviors.[1]

As you begin, this three-step approach is both useful and effective.

Need for and Uses of a New Skill

Back in 1964, a bestselling book, *Games People Play,* by Dr. Eric Berne, alerted the public and the business world to the need of improving employee's interpersonal skills. Berne theorized that, on the average, 55% to 85% of employees' time was wasted playing *games* which he defined as destructive, non-productive interactions between people in which the real purpose of the interaction was not to achieve a productive goal but for one or both "players" in the game to realize some ulterior motive or satisfy some personality need. Berne identified over 90 games that people play and many of these apply primarily to business organizations. Here are a few of them:

Why don't you ... Yes, but ...

- Played by people or groups who appear to want others to help them solve their problems.

- The initiator rejects all suggestions with reasons why the advice will not work, proving that, "No one can tell me what to do."

Kick Me

- In this game the player does something to provoke another player to criticize him or otherwise make him feel inferior.

- They tend to attract opposite players who will take advantage.
  "My report is late." (*I'm a bad person.*)
  "Again?" *"You know I needed that report today."* (*Yes, you are a bad person, and here is your kick.*)

Now I've Got You

- This is a game in which a person tries to trap another in a mistake, lie, or other negative situation.

- If successful in trapping his victim, the player feels justified in taking some negative action: firing someone, not giving a raise, or writing a critical report.
  "Did you finish typing that letter I gave you this morning?"
  (Noticing it is still in the typewriter.)
  "Er ... Yes, sir."
  "Oh?" *"What's this then?"*

Other Business Games

- *Blemish:* A supervisor finds major fault with a minor mistake.

- *Bear Trap:* A supervisor coaxes an employee into doing a report, then overwhelms him with size and complexity of the job.

Games not only interfere with honest, meaningful social relationships, but they also get in the way of productivity and are obstacles to individuals and organizations reaching their goals.

Berne succeeded in ringing the warning bell loud enough so

that further research followed. It became quickly apparent that skilled communicators wasted less time reaching their objectives and were more productive. When interpersonal communication skills improved, managers managed better and employees responded more enthusiastically. In other words, work became more productive, satisfying, and rewarding in direct relation to the improvement of interpersonal communication skills.

Identifying the Behaviors Involved in the New Skill

In 1969, five years after the publication of *Games People Play*, Bruno Bettelheim wrote that the person well-trained in interpersonal communication should be able to 1/ relate successfully to self and others, 2/ analyze personal and environmental experiences and make inferences from them for future behavior, 3/ understand self well enough to develop and maintain an individual sense of identity, and 4/ respond to life situations in accordance with his/her own interests, values, and beliefs without being aware of or insensitive to the values, interests, and beliefs of others.[2]

Twelve years later, in 1981, David Johnson stated that the interpersonal skills that needed to be developed were:

  1/ knowing and trusting each other
  2/ developing open and honest communication
  3/ accepting and supporting each other, and
  4/ resolving conflicts and relationship problems
      constructively[3]

Two themes emerge from the recent research about interpersonal communication. An individual must have a positive self-image and be sincerely interested in another person or persons before he can effectively communicate to another. These basic principles of interpersonal communication apply to our social relationships as well as our business relationships, so there is a dual reason to work at them. However, our main concern in this text is *how* to improve interpersonal skills that will lead to career success. Here are some ways to do that:

1/ Putting Interpersonal Behaviors Into Practice:
   Be Other-Oriented

One central truth of all interpersonal transactions is that you must be genuinely concerned and interested in the person with whom you are communicating. You must be empathetic. That is, you must try to understand the other person's point of view or, to use the cliché, "put yourself in the other person's shoes." To do this requires discipline because it is our natural inclination to impose our own viewpoint on someone else. This natural tendency leads to blocked communication which is essentially time-wasting. Open the channels to let ideas flow both ways. This open-minded approach leads to mutual respect and trust which, in turn, leads to productivity.

2/ Understand the Objective of the Communication

Knowing the true purpose of communication is vital to successful interpersonal exchanges. What is it you are trying to accomplish? Is it your purpose to pass on information or are you trying to motivate another person? Once the purpose is clarified, the methods of communication will follow logically. Your choice of tone, language, and approach will suit the situation. For example, the purpose of a job interview is clear: you want to be offered a job. To accomplish that objective, there are very specific things you need to do to make that happen. (See section on interviewing skills in PART V.)

3/ Choose a Proper Setting for the Communication

This is an often overlooked yet crucial point about communication. Two people with the best of intentions can have their communication spoiled by choosing the wrong time and place to interact or communicating in a place which is not suited to the productive exchange of ideas. Don't expect to be well received if you stop a person in the street or in a hallway or crowded meeting to discuss issues of importance. Even an otherwise ideal office environment can be spoiled by telephones, radios, or other people as distractions.

Instead, be certain that both parties have ample time to devote to the issue being discussed. (This eliminates the furtive glancing at watches or wall clocks which is the death blow to communications.) Eliminate distractions. If it is your office, hold the telephone calls and ask not to be disturbed. Make your visitor feel comfortable and relaxed and assure him that he is important enough to receive your exclusive attention for a period of time. *For example,* "Mary, you and I have an hour to discuss this suggestion of yours before my next appointment. Let's see what we can do to make your ideas become company policy."

4/ Clarify Your Thoughts Before You Speak

In our culture many of us seem uncomfortable with the silence that accompanies pauses in conversation. As a result, too often we rush to fill the void with words that we have not carefully considered. The result can be a disaster. Think before you speak. Once your ideas are together, express them as best you can.

5/ *Seek the Advice of Others*

One of the nicest compliments you can pay another person is to ask their opinion or advice on a subject. It tells the other person you value them and their ideas. Try it. Not only will you have made someone feel good, but you just might learn something of value. Should this happen, be certain to give credit where it is due and let the person know you are appreciative of their contribution.

6/ *Think of Tomorrow, Not Just Today*

Most of your interactions with people in business are ongoing. That is, you are likely to have continuing relationships with the same people over extended periods of time. Remember that and avoid the "Christmas Party" scene where, after a few glasses of punch have loosened the tongue, employees have been known to tell their associates (or supervisors) just what they "really" think of them. The next day always arrives and, with it, feelings of regret and remorse. Go easy on the emotions and try to cultivate relationships that will be satisfying and productive.

7/ The last suggestions for effective interpersonal communication are to **Listen Well** and to **Be Aware of the Nonverbal Means of Communication.** These two areas of communication are so important that we have devoted entire units to them which follow.

A final word on interpersonal communication: there is probably nothing as important to your happiness and success as being able to get along well with other people both in your private and business lives. *Work at doing it well.*

3

LISTENING

The communication skill that has been the "hottest" item in our culture in recent years is listening. The combination of scholarly research into listening and the attention focused on it by major corporations has changed the way we think about the skill. No longer do we take listening for granted as a process that happens instinctively as long as we are able to hear. We know better now. No longer do businesses concentrate only on training their employees to speak and write more effectively. Today, typical employee seminars include training sessions on how to become better listeners. The best example of this interesting blend of academic findings and corporate concerns took place at the Sperry Corp., a large multinational corporation with 87,000 employees in 33 countries. The story is a logical place to begin as you start thinking about your own listening skills. After all, if the management of a corporate giant with annual sales of $4.2 billion a year considers listening important, there must be something to it.

**The Sperry
Story**

In the fall of 1979, Sperry launched an external advertising program and an internal training program based on the importance of effective listening. In the first three years, the listening message appeared on television and in magazines and newspapers with a combined circulation of more than 65.5 million in America and 10.5 million in Europe. The central message of the advertising campaign was that Sperry employees work at listening and responding and that Sperry had made listening a fundamental philosophy of doing business. Sperry's chairman and chief executive, J. Paul Lyet, was so serious about the program that he delayed the start of the advertising campaign six months until the employee training seminars in listening skills were well underway. The seminars were designed with the assistance of Lyman K. Steil, Chairman of the Speech Communications Division at the University of Minnesota and a consultant to more than 300 corporations and government agencies.

On the following pages, you'll see three of those ads that proved to be so effective.

From the beginning, the senior management at Sperry stated that the commitment to listening would be long term and, indeed, it continues to this day. Their motivation was clear. Improved listening would ultimately result in higher efficiency, increased productivity, and an improved company image. The company diverted thousands of man-hours to classroom training on listening skills at each of its five divisions.

In addition, internal mailings of 55,000 specially prepared phonograph recordings and accompanying pamphlets sent the message to employees throughout the world. To date, approximately *25,000* employees have been trained and the effort continues.

What significance does the Sperry story have for young men and women who are planning careers in business? The answer to that question is simple. If the people at Sperry "understand how important it is to listen," you should too. *Begin now to learn how to become a more effective listener.*

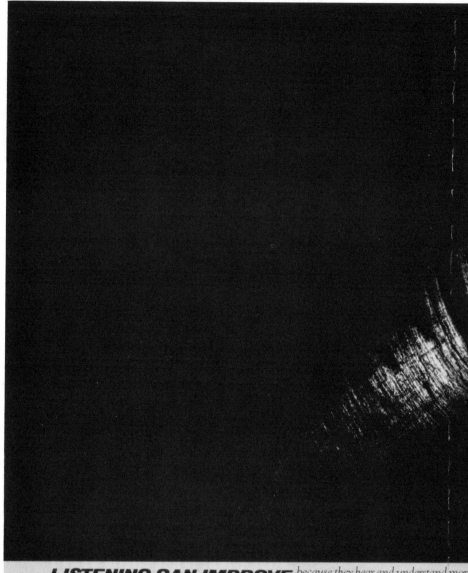

LISTENING CAN IMPROVE YOUR VISION.

Few, we've found, see as far or as clearly as those who listen well.

Good listeners think more broadly— because they hear and understand mor facts and points of view.

They make better innovators. Because listeners look at problems with fresh eyes, combine what they learn in more unlikely w they're more apt to hit upon truly startling id

Ultimately, good listeners attune

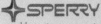

IT PAYS TO LISTEN.

Columbus' ideas fell on deaf ears for years
before Queen Isabella finally chose to listen.
It's a lesson that wasn't lost on Sperry.
Listening keeps us alert to ever-expanding

possibilities in computer science, aerospace
and defense.
What's more, it helps us expand them
ourselves.
Real breakthroughs increasingly occur
when seemingly unrelated advances get co
nected—and then, suddenly, explosively fus
This takes an attentive, imaginative k.
of listener who combines the unlikely in

xpected ways.

It's why, at Sperry's Research Center,
ntists from eighteen totally different disci-
es regularly meet.

To listen to each other.

We at Sperry are convinced that listening
ignites new insights, guides us into

uncharted areas of thought, and ultimately
uncovers whole new worlds.

We understand how important it is to listen.

What We Have Learned About Listening

Many of the new ideas and attitudes about listening are a result of the new knowledge we have acquired about the skill. Research has proven that the old thinking about listening contained many contradictions and misconceptions. One obvious contradiction is that even though we spend a greater percentage of our waking hours listening (45%) than we do the other communication skills (writing (9%), reading (16%), and speaking (30%)), we devote the least amount of time (8%) to classroom teaching of the skill (reading gets 52% of classroom time).[4] Do you remember the last instruction you received in listening?

A very common misconception most people have is that they are skilled listeners. The exact opposite is true. Most people are poor listeners, and this lack of skill often causes problems in their professional and personal lives.

"The cost of wasted time, wasted productivity, broken-down relationships, injury, death and lawsuits all come about because Party A sends a message to Party B and Party B may not respond to it or interpret it," states Lyman Steil.

"If you ask someone to listen to a short message that runs 10 minutes in length and then ask what the person heard, what was evaluated, retained and what the person could respond to, he would operate at about the 50% mark."

"If you come back in 48 hours and test again," Steil continues, "he'll drop down to the 25% effectiveness level."[5] These figures of 50% retention (immediate) and 25% retention (after 48 hours) confirmed by testing are far below what people normally rate as their own listening effectiveness.

As the contradictions and misconceptions are clarified, a brighter side of the picture emerges. *Anyone can become a better listener.* That positive note is reinforced by Dr. Ralph G. Nichols who researched, published, and taught in the area of listening for 35 years and claimed: "Listening is a collection of identifiable skills. It can be improved through training and practice, just as reading, writing, and speaking."[6] This is what the seminars at Sperry Corp. are about and what the rest of this unit is concerned with: improving listening skills. The benefits, both in your professional and personal lives, are worth it.

What Causes Ineffective Listening

People are not listening-oriented beings. Our society rewards those people who write and speak well and, as a consequence, our educational system devotes countless hours of training to perfect these skills. We do not customarily associate listening with success and almost no time is spent developing proficiency as listeners. The result is that few people develop strong listening skills.

Most people are egocentric: that is, they tend to be self-centered and want to put their own wishes and desires first. Writing and speaking allow them to assert their own personalities in an active way that satisfies the needs of their ego. On the other hand, listening requires that we be other-oriented, that we temporarily place the needs and concerns of another person in front of our own. When our ego prevents us from doing this, it becomes an obstacle to effective listening.

A very common cause of poor listening is daydreaming which is the primary alternative to listening. Our minds wander from the subject at hand and travel to other times and places which often have no connection with the present. The reason we indulge our favorite fantasies rather than listen is because we are able to comprehend spoken words at a rate of 500 words per minute. Since the average speaker talks at a rate of 125-250 words per minute, we are left with a great deal of free time in which to daydream. If we do not use this free time productively, our listening will suffer as a result.

Distractions are the next major cause of poor listening. In order to listen effectively, you must concentrate your attention on the speaker and what is being said. Anything that breaks that concentration interferes with the listening process. Ringing telephones, people interruptions, typewriters, radios, and other office noises are all examples of potential distractions. In other words, an inappropriate environment can impede listening.

Finally, there are some poor behavioral habits which create blocks to effective listening. Most of these come from our attitudes toward the speaker and the subject. If, for example, we don't like the speaker or the way he or she looks, we may tune out and miss some valuable content. If we react with anger or any excessive emotion to what is said, we may miss the message. If we have preconceptions that material may be too easy or too difficult, we may close our minds to important information. Covering our ears is a physical act that can prevent hearing. In much the same way, we often "cover" our minds with psychological barriers that prevent listening.

**Problems
Resulting
From
Ineffective
Listening**

The cost of poor listening in our society is very great. White collar workers spend 40% of their time listening and top management even more. Beside the obvious damage to productivity caused by a lack of listening, the University of Minnesota contends that 60% of misunderstandings in business are caused by poor listening. Another recent study ranked listening second as the communication problem most identified by subordinates as leading to ineffective communication incidents.[7] The *Harvard Business Review* addressed the problem bluntly: "the biggest block to personal communication is man's ability to listen."

Not all the costs of poor listening can be measured in economic terms. Poor listening damages relationships between husbands and wives, parents and children, and friends. Today the United States has the dubious distinction of having the highest divorce rate in the modern world. Each year approximately 50% as many couples get divorced as get married. One of the major contributing factors to the spiraling divorce rate is a failure of partners to communicate with and listen to each other. We can say then that the inability to listen effectively not only hurts us in our careers but in our interpersonal relationships as well.

**Benefits From
Improved
Listening**

It follows that improved listening skills should produce worthwhile results, and they do. Robert Montgomery, a respected professional speaker who has trained more than 150,000 people in communication skills, states matter-of-factly that if working people were taught to listen effectively, the efficiency of American business could be doubled.[8] Misunderstandings and the problems that result are minimized. Managers manage more effectively and their subordinates react more positively when they sense an atmosphere of mutual trust. Quality information flows more freely through open communication channels allowing for better decision making by management and clearer understanding of policies and objectives by employees. In short, improved listening contributes to productivity which leads to success.

Business success is not the only by-product of improved listening. An equally predictable benefit is that better listening will have a direct effect on the day-to-day relationships we have with others in our social lives. Think for a moment about a friend or acquaintance whom you enjoy being with more than others. Consider the characteristics of that person's personality you enjoy. Chances are that among the traits you find appealing will be the fact that the person listens to you when you talk. ***GOOD LISTENERS ARE POPULAR PEOPLE.*** Further than that, effective listening tends to create reciprocal behavior in the other person. That is, after a person has been attentive and listened to what you have to say, it is natural for you to do the same in return. That, of course, is effective communication. The potential positive effect of improved listening on marriages, parent-child relationships, and friendships is enormous. *Try it. It works.*

How to Be a Better Listener

Psychological Changes:

Becoming a better listener requires psychological as well as behavioral changes. First, you must accept the fact that *everyone* can become a more skilled listener if he or she has the *desire* to do so. Improvement doesn't just happen; it happens to those who want it to happen and are willing to work hard to see that it does. Second, you must be willing to adopt a new attitude about the act of listening. Put aside the old idea that listening is just a *passive* act that occurs naturally if you are able to hear. Instead, think of listening as an *active* behavior which requires an expenditure of energy just as does writing or speaking. Consider listening as hard work for that is what it is. Third, you must understand that effective listening requires that you suppress your ego and become *other-oriented*. This is quite difficult as it seems natural to think of ourselves first; we know, however, that this is a block to listening and so we must, for a time, put the person we are listening to first and try to accept and understand that person as he/she is. Once you are able to make these three psychological adjustments, you are ready to tackle the behavioral changes necessary to effective listening.

Behavioral Changes:

A dialogue is defined as an open and frank interchange and discussion of ideas between people while a monologue refers to the remarks of someone speaking alone. No doubt, you are familiar with these terms. Are you, however, familiar with the term "duologue?" "Duologue" is the tongue-in-cheek term given to a most common obstacle to listening, two people talking at the same time. It is so common as to be epidemic, and yet, the cure is painless. All you have to do is ***STOP TALKING,*** and ***LISTEN*** *to the speaker's entire message without interrupting.* Lyndon Johnson made this point quite well when he said, "If you're talking; you aren't learning."

Another crucial factor in listening is the place or environment in which communication takes place. To the extent that it is possible, you should *try to create a comfortable, relaxed atmosphere from which distractions have been removed.* Specifically, this may mean many things. Put the speaker at ease by having him/her sit down; don't stand over a speaker who is sitting; hold the telephone calls and ask not to be interrupted; seek a quiet spot which is appropriate for communication. Even though space is often at a premium in active businesses, individuals can take extra steps to make their space suitable to interpersonal communication and listening.

Earlier you learned that listeners are able to understand words at a rate of 500 words per minute while the average speaker talks at a rate of 125-250 words per minute. If you *learn how to use this resulting free time wisely,* you can become a better listener. Rather than daydreaming or thinking of what you are going to say next, discipline yourself to mentally summarize what is being said, relate it to what you already know about the subject, question or evaluate the message, and be mindful of nonverbal clues that the speaker may be sending.

This nonverbal aspect of communication is one of a listener's major responsibilities. *You must show the speaker that you are willing to listen.* The ways to do that are to appear attentive by assuming an interested posture (leaning toward the speaker is a sign of interest) and a receptive facial expression. Another way to show a willingness to listen is to maintain eye contact during communication. In our culture, it is considered normal for people to look at each other 40% to 60% of the time during communication. More than the normal amount of eye contact indicates increased interest while less than normal eye contact indicates disinterest on the part of the listener. Strive for 80 to 90% eye contact when listening.

Besides nonverbal feedback, the listener can and should *provide oral feedback* during pauses by the speaker. Restate the basic ideas to be sure you have understood correctly, and ask questions which help the speaker elaborate and clarify his/her ideas.

Finally, we can become better listeners if *we are optimistic, open-minded listeners who refrain from negativism and emotional reactions.* Expect the best of people until proven otherwise. Be willing to accept the views of others and don't always try to change them to your own ways. It won't work so save your energy. You may not like a speaker's personality but that same person may know something of value to you. Be aware of your own biases and preconceptions so that you are able to minimize emotional reactions except when they are appropriate. Doing these things is not the same thing as saying you must *agree* with every speaker's point-of-view. That is not the case. What is being said is that, before you dismiss or disagree with another point-of-view, you must first listen to it fairly and with an open mind.

Conclusion

You are ready now to put into practice what you have learned about listening. First, you will have an opportunity to do so in the Exercises and Activities that follow. These are, out of necessity, simulated exercises whose purpose it is to reinforce effective listening skills. Ultimately, it is up to you and your willingness to try out the new ideas in your everyday encounters with family, fellow workers, friends, and teachers that will decide whether you will be a better listener. If you do, you will have acquired another communication skill that will contribute to your career success.

Listening Exercises

I/ Divide the class into triads (3 students in a group). Participants in each triad should designate themselves A, B, or C. Topics for discussion are listed below. In each triad, one person should act as referee and the other two as participants in a discussion of one of the topics found on the sheet. One will be the speaker and the other the listener. Here are the rules for the exercise:

1/ The discussion is to be unstructured except that before each participant speaks, he or she must first summarize, in his or her own words and without notes, what has been said previously.

2/ The speaker and the referee are free to interrupt if they feel that the summary is inaccurate.

3/ Participant A begins as speaker, choosing a topic from the list.

4/ Participant B will be the listener and Participant C the referee.

5/ Each discussion should last for 3 minutes.

6/ Participant B now becomes the speaker, C the listener, and A the referee. B chooses a new topic and the discussion proceeds.

7/ After 3 more minutes, the triads stop and change roles. C is now the speaker, A the listener, and B the referee.

8/ After three or four rounds of discussion, members of the triads should share feelings and reactions to the exercise by responding to the following questions:

a/ Which role was the most difficult?

b/ Did you find you were not getting across what you wanted to say?

c/ Did you have difficulty listening to others during the exercise?

Topics for Discussion for Triads

What is success?

Describe the ideal man.

Describe the ideal woman.

Why are divorces increasing in the U.S.?

Do you believe life exists elsewhere in the universe?

Should women be allowed to fight in combat?

What should be the legal drinking age?

Why are people prejudiced?

What is the most difficult sport to play?

II/ Write a paragraph replying to these questions:

　　a/ How do you know when someone is not listening to you? How does it make you feel?

　　b/ What do I have to do to become a good listener?

NONVERBAL COMMUNICATION

There is a humorous story told about President Franklin Delano Roosevelt who decided to liven up a tiresome White House receiving line one evening. As each guest came up and said, "Good evening, Mr. President, how are you, sir?" Roosevelt responded warmly with a pleasant smile and a firm handshake, "Fine, thank you, I just murdered my mother-in-law." Not one person going through the receiving line reacted to his comment. It's doubtful people even heard it.[9] What is clear from this anecdote is that President Roosevelt was ahead of his time in his instinctive understanding of the power of nonverbal communication or body language. He knew his guests would pay more attention to his handshake, facial expression, and the tone of his voice than to the words he actually said. Today, through research in *kinesics,* the study of bodily movements and other nonverbal means of communication, we are more acutely aware of this important aspect of communication and how it contributes to success in business.

From your earliest years, parents and teachers have stressed the importance of learning the spoken language. Large amounts of time and energy are spent mastering language. When we work at using language properly, we choose our words consciously and carefully. Also, we place a high social value on using words well, and we often reward people who are skilled in language use with positions of power and/or prestige. By comparison, we devote relatively little time to learning about nonverbal communication and, as a result, this part of our overall communication system often operates without direction. If, however, we pay attention to the findings of Albert Mehrabian who conducted tests to determine how much body, voice, and words contributed to the total impact of a person's attitudes, we find we may have our priorities backward. Take this opportunity to take your own guess by penciling in the percentages you think apply:

Total Impact Theory:

Body & other nonverbal	_50_ %
Voice	_30_ %
Words (Verbal)	_20_ %
	100%

Mehrabian's research indicated these results: body and other nonverbal, 55%; voice, 38%; and words (verbal), 7%. Are you surprised? If so, then you need to learn more about nonverbal communication.

While our verbal communication refers to the words that we use, nonverbal communication is more broad-based. It includes tone of voice, facial expression, eye contact, body posture, gestures, body movement, physical appearance including dress, and use of space. Because we have been trained for years to use language, we can manipulate and disguise our verbal messages with ease. The same is not true for the nonverbal channels. Our bodies are predisposed to convey only the true meaning of our expressions. This causes problems for when there is a conflict between verbal and nonverbal messages, the listener will rely on the nonverbal message, confirming the old truism that actions speak louder than words. Knowing this, you can see that there are two major benefits to be gained through knowledge of nonverbal communication. First, as receivers of communication *(listeners)*, we can look for evidence that will help us understand more fully the message of the speaker. Second, as communicators *(speakers)*, we can take steps to be sure that our nonverbal behavior is supportive of the words we choose to say.

Listen With Your Eyes As Well As Your Ears

In the previous unit, you learned that an essential part of listening is to be mindful of nonverbal clues. To be a more alert communicator, you must *see* the message as well as hear it. Seeing nonverbal messages is one thing; interpreting them is quite another and requires some knowledge of generally accepted nonverbal principles. A word of caution at the outset; nonverbal signs often may be interpreted in more than one way and this makes the task of "reading" them more difficult. For example, if a person attempts to get very close to another person, it may be a sign of warm feelings of friendship or, in another context, it might mean provocation or aggression. For this reason, you must be alert to both verbal and nonverbal messages and notice if they are consistent with one another or if there is a conflict. Also, one nonverbal sign by itself may be meaningless. Taken together with two or three other nonverbal messages, the message may suddenly become very clear. Following are some common nonverbal signals and what they might mean.

Reading Nonverbal Signs

It is known that facial expressions and bodily movements provide clues to attitudes and feelings that are normally concealed. The eyes indicate surprise and disgust and/or frustration are signaled by a person's mouth. Even if people try to hide these feelings, small, fleeting changes provide insights into the true feelings of the individual. Open-mindedness is reflected by open hands and an unbuttoned coat while defensiveness is indicated by arms crossed over the chest, crossed legs, and aggressive gestures. If a person is suspicious, he or she may glance sideways, rub the nose or eyes, button a coat and move away from another individual. People of higher status indulge in more relaxed and expansive postures; for example, a manager might lean back in a chair with feet on a desk when talking with a subordinate. The subordinate, on the other hand, signals his secondary status by sitting upright and appearing attentive. As mentioned in the previous unit, a less than normal amount of eye contact clearly suggests disinterest or boredom while the opposite is true.

Wringing of hands, rubbing the back of the neck or running hands through the hair are seen as signs of frustration, while biting fingernails and chewing pens or pencils indicate insecurity. Nervousness is shown openly by clearing your throat, smoking, covering your mouth with your hand as you speak, jingling pocket money, tugging at your ear, fidgeting in your chair, and not looking at the other person. By contrast, the confident person will often sit up straight, place his hands in coat pockets with the thumbs out, or place hands behind the back. A final category of body movements shows you are thinking something over or evaluating a matter; stroking your chin, tilting your head, hand-to-face gestures, peering over your glasses, taking your glasses off or cleaning them, and putting your hand to the bridge of the nose, are some of these.[10]

**The Use of
Space**

Paying attention to nonverbal signals also means noting the space between participants in a communication transaction. Research has revealed that the space between participants in communication depends on the *nature* of the communication. Our personal space reaches out to 1½ feet from us and is reserved only for those with whom we have an intimate relationship. Friendly, casual relationships take place between 1½ and 4 feet. The rest of our communications, impersonal and secondary relationships, occur outside of 4 feet. Americans, in particular, are sensitive to the use of space and feel uncomfortable when they are placed in situations where these informal space restrictions are violated. You can see proof of this the next time you ride in a crowded elevator. The people in the elevator will be uncomfortable because their private space has been entered by strangers who they are forced to stand close to for the duration of the ride. They will show their discomfort by staring at the floor or at the floor indicator on the door of the elevator in strained, embarrassed silence. Handshakes and other forms of touching dissolve interpersonal space and may signal a willingness to explore a more personal relationship. There is still much that we have to learn about this aspect of human communication.

The message is clear. As you begin to further develop your communication skills, you need to see the message as well as hear it. Remember the caution that one nonverbal signal may be ambiguous, easy to misinterpret. Look for a number of signs which together, may provide additional insight into the speaker. Finally, be cautious of those who would manipulate others through the use of nonverbal communication.

**Controlling
Your
Nonverbal
Messages**

Next, it is necessary to learn how to use your knowledge of nonverbal communication as an asset that will help in business and social relationships. The word *asset* is used deliberately for, to be sure, the person insensitive or unaware of nonverbal communication can certainly create a *liability* that will work against success. You can offend or antagonize others and create a negative image of yourself just as easily without words as you can with words. Contemporary historians agree that it wasn't Richard Nixon's words that lost him the televised debates to John F. Kennedy during the presidential campaign of 1960. Nixon's words were fine; it was his appearance, the nonverbal messages that came across to the television audience that cost him the debates and, possibly, the election.

To be truly effective as a communicator, you must not only be skilled verbally and nonverbally, but you must make both messages *consistent* with each other. Remember when inconsistency occurs, the listener will rely on the nonverbal message and the transmission of this kind of missed or contradictory message will give an overall negative feeling to the communication. With this key point in mind, here are some suggestions on how to make your own nonverbal communication work for you.

Managing Your Nonverbal Signals

Eye Contact:

Dorothy Sarnoff, a communications consultant whose clients have included presidents as well as leaders of business, stresses the importance of eye contact this way. "Speaking without eye contact is like talking with a bag over your head."[11] You need to know that your eyes convey messages of approval, love, interest, sincerity, credibility, enthusiasm, excitement — and all of the negative emotions as well. Be aware that it is eye contact that projects confidence and trust and, conversely, the lack of eye contact suggests a negative self-image, feelings of inferiority, and even a neurotic personality. Work at maintaining eye contact 80%-90% of the time during a communication without staring.

Americans are not comfortable when others stare at them; if you wish to test the truth of this statement, begin staring at a stranger as he or she approaches you on a sidewalk. Within seconds, the stranger will feel uncomfortable and suspect that something is wrong. You don't have to stare to use your eyes effectively. Look directly at a person, but move your eyes so that they do not linger too long on the same point of focus. Later, in the chapter on Public Speaking, you will learn how important it is to sweep your eyes across your audience in order to be effective. The same principle of the importance of eye contact applies also to one-on-one interpersonal exchanges.

Facial Expressions:

During a few of your next classes, look around at the faces of your teachers and your classmates. What messages are being signaled by their facial expressions? If yours are typical classes, you will see expressions of interest and enthusiasm as well as those of disinterest and weariness. Which of the people seem more alive, more appealing? Can't you tell, without hearing a word that is spoken, who is really involved and who is more likely to be benefiting from the class? What messages are you sending by the expression on your face?

Cultivate a habit now that will help you in your business career. Let your face come alive and tell the world that you enjoy what you are doing. Smile and show acceptance and interest when appropriate. Enthusiasm is contagious but people need to know you have it before they can catch it.

Posture and Gestures:

Some people seem to have more "presence" than others. When they walk into a room, they make an immediate impact. Often, the explanation for this quality is in the physical appearance or manner of dress of an individual. However, part of that same impact is explained by body posture and gestures, the way a person sits or stands and the hand movements that accompany the spoken message. They key word here is "energy". You need to feel that you are spending energy by maintaining a fairly erect posture, leaning forward and using natural hand gestures that add to or complement the words you are speaking. Above all else, avoid a slumping, sagging body posture and hand motions that distract the attention of the listener from your message.

Other points to help you manage your nonverbal signals are:

1. Try to maintain a reasonable distance of four to six feet during your business exchanges and realize that most people feel uncomfortable when their personal space is invaded.

2. Speak at a reasonable pace so your listener will have no difficulty understanding you and vary the tone of your voice to avoid a tiresome monotone.

3. It is obvious that your clothing and overall personal appearance should be suited to the occasion. Studies have indicated that when dress and appearance are inconsistent with position — say, a male banker who has long hair, a beard, and wears casual clothing to his office — people are less trustful and unwilling to place confidence in that person.

If you are already practicing positive nonverbal behavior, continue doing so. If you have acquired habits that will work against your own success, it will not be an easy task to change them. You will need to work at each point until new habits are established. Remember the key point. Your verbal and nonverbal messages should be consistent with each other, and, when they are not, listeners will rely on the nonverbal signals for the truth and the overall impression will be negative.

Non-Verbal Exercises

I/ Describe in detail the appropriate non-verbal behaviors in which you might engage during a typical face-to-face interaction with another person. Be sure to provide details about all the non-verbal sign systems — eye contact, posture, spatial orientation, gestures, and tone and pace of delivery. Your instructions are for a visitor from another planet who is beginning his business career.

II/ Write a short essay which discusses some of the benefits as well as the possible problems of learning more about non-verbal behavior.

III/ Write a description of the environment in which you do most of your communicating. Is the environment helpful to communication and, if not, what can you do to change it?

Endnotes

1 *Reaching Out: Interpersonal Effectiveness and Self-Actualization* by David W. Johnson.

2 *Reaching Out: Interpersonal Effectiveness and Self-Actualization* by David W. Johnson.

3 *Reaching Out: Interpersonal Effectiveness and Self-Actualization* by David W. Johnson.

4 *Perceptive Listening* by Florence Wolff, Nadine C. Marsnik, William S. Jacey, and Ralph G. Nichols.

5 "Most People Found to Be Poor Listeners" by Dolores Barclay in the *Providence Journal*.

6 *Perceptive Listening* by Florence Wolff, Nadine C. Marsnik, William S. Jacey, and Ralph G. Nichols.

7 "A Field Study of Listening Needs in Organizations" by Gary T. Hunt and Louis P. Cunsella.

8 *Listening Made Easy* by Robert L. Montgomery.

9 *Effective Communication on the Job* by William K. Fallon.

10 *Listening Made Easy* by Robert L. Montgomery.

11 *Make the Most of Your Best* by Dorothy Sarnoff.

Public Speaking for Business

5 |||||||||

PUBLIC SPEAKING FOR BUSINESS

Of all the communication skills that you need to master, perhaps none is more challenging and demanding than presenting a speech to a group of people. Unlike the other skills, speech-making requires you to stand alone on "center stage" before an audience whose entire attention is focused on you. To be effective takes much planning and practice, but the rewards to be gained are certainly worth the effort. There is no more effective way to favorably impress a number of people with your knowledge, personality, and ability to communicate than by presenting an effective speech. The opposite of this is equally true. Which impression you make will depend on how hard you work to learn and put into practice the ideas in the chapter. One thing is *certain*. Once your career in business begins, you will have the opportunity to speak in front of a group much sooner than you may think.

Most of you will be required to give speeches or "talks" before groups as part of your job responsibilities. Many of you will begin very early in your careers. As is discussed in a later chapter (The Corporation — A New Way of Life), most companies have established rituals which are followed faithfully year after year. One of the favorite corporate rituals is to have new employees give a short speech to fellow employees at a business meeting or social function. It is a convenient way for the established employees to become acquainted with and to form impressions of new arrivals. The newcomer is generally asked to present a brief biography and to share first impressions of the new job with the group. The ritual is a kind of *initiation* and how you perform can either ease your acceptance into the new group or make it more difficult.

There are many other occasions when you will be asked to speak before groups. The types of situations you will face will depend on your chosen occupation. Here are some other possibilities.

Speeches to:

- meetings as a fill-in for a superior

- a group of visitors touring your place of business

- the local Chamber of Commerce on behalf of your firm

- a group of fellow employees explaining new office procedures or changes in fringe benefit programs

- a college or high school class who requested a representative from your company

- church groups, school board meetings, city council meetings, and zoning commission meetings

- union meetings

These are just a few of many possible occasions where you may be asked to talk publicly. Does all of this sound a bit frightening? Do you feel some anxiety when you think of yourself having to stand alone in front of an audience? If the answers to these two questions is "yes," it simply means that you are perfectly normal. That very normal problem is labeled "speech anxiety" or, as some others call it, "stage fright." In 1977, *The Book of Lists* reported that Americans' foremost fear was fear of speaking before a group which beat out heights, insects and bugs, and even death to become our number one phobia. More recent surveys have confirmed those findings including an informal ten-year poll of students at a northeastern business college in which 75% (approximately 2,270 students) listed speaking in front of others as their major communications concern. Because the problem is so common and because speech anxiety can interfere with effective speech making unless properly managed, you must first learn to understand and overcome it.

OVERCOMING SPEECH ANXIETY

Just the idea of having to stand up and talk before an audience can cause many different types of responses within you. Some of these are psychological; others are physiological. One student, obviously suffering from an extreme attack of stage fright, summed up the physiological responses in the following way:

> What's wrong with me? I'm losing control. My heart is racing, my head is pounding; my face is on fire; my hands are cold and shaking; my knees are twitching; I can't stop sweating; my stomach is in a knot; my muscles are stiffening up on me, and I can't breathe. Please help me. I think I'm flipping out!

It is highly unlikely that your symptoms of speech anxiety will be as extreme as those described above, but you *can* expect some reactions with lesser degrees of intensity which will depend on a variety of other variables. Recognize these symptoms for what they are, the result of stress build-up and self-induced fear. Remember that these feelings are natural and widely shared by others. Through this understanding and through practice before your classmates, you can become "desensitized" to the problem. *You can learn how to cope and manage your fear of public speaking.*

What happens when an anxiety attack or "flipping out" episode strikes you? Dr. Herbert Benson, M.D., Associate Professor of Medicine at Harvard Medical School and Director of the Division of Behavioral Medicine at Boston's Beth Israel Hospital, tells us in his best selling book, *The Relaxation Response,* that people ". . . react in a predictable way to acute and chronic stressful situations, which triggers an inborn response that has been part of our physiologic makeup for perhaps millions of years. This has been popularly labeled the 'fight-or-flight' response." This response then, is a natural, instinctual reaction due to the build-up of stress and fear over a speaking assignment. Putting it simply, extra adrenalin is being released and increases in your blood pressure, heart rate, rate of breathing, and blood flow to the muscles and metabolism are taking place. You are now ready to stand for a "fight" or prepared to run or "flight." Obviously your speaking assignment hardly warrants a "fight" or "flight," but it is hard to tell your body not to respond that way. No wonder you feel uneasy about your speech requirements.

What can be done to control your nervous responses? More often than not very simple recommendations will help you. Being prepared is the best single suggestion for speech makers. Dale Carnegie, the famous speech teacher, taught his students that preparation is the key. He believed that "only the prepared speaker deserves to be confident.'' James Harvey Robinson in his book, *The Mind in the Making,* states: ''It is fear that holds us back. And fear is begotten of ignorance and uncertainty.'' Fear is overcome by thorough preparation. By complete planning beforehand, you will have something to say and you will be prepared. The Boy Scouts' motto, ''Be prepared,'' is on target for the speech maker.

Rehearsing the speech before caring and constructive critics will decrease your apprehension. A good listener can reinforce your good points and help you ''smooth the rough edges.'' Perhaps you can enlist the help of a roommate, some friends, or a family member. Talk the speech through with someone else. The practice will increase your confidence and make you more familiar with the content. Again, you will be decreasing any uncertainty about the speech.

Always recall that a certain amount of nervous energy is a good thing and that you are in good company. Many public figures have experienced stage fright. Show business people like Johnny Carson, Merv Griffin, Jimmy Stewart, Sidney Poitier, Dinah Shore, and Carol Burnett, have all been quoted as suffering from ''nerves.'' Carroll O'Connor of *All in the Family* and *Archie's Place* said this:

> A professional actor has a kind of tension. The amateur is thrown by it but the professional needs it.

Political figures have not been immune from stage fright either: Sir Winston Churchill and Presidents Reagan, Carter, Ford, Nixon, Johnson, Kennedy, Eisenhower, and Truman all showed nervous signs in their speeches. Even the famous Roman orator, Cicero, said: ''I turn pale at the outset of a speech and quake in every limb and in all my soul.'' However, none of these men let their apprehensions stop them from succeeding. They were *determined* to perform for their audiences.

Try to channel your extra nervous energy into the delivery of your speech. Use your energy enthusiastically and remember that you are stronger than your anxieties. It is reassuring to note that most of the things that you worry about never materialize. If you *behave* confidently, you just may begin to *feel* confident. The famous American psychologist, William James, put it well when he wrote:

> Action seems to follow feeling, but really action and feeling go together; and by regulating the action, which is under the mere direct control of the will, we

can indirectly regulate the feeling, which is not.

Thus the sovereign voluntary path to cheerfulness, if our spontaneous cheerfulness be lost, is to sit up cheerfully and to act and speak as if cheerfulness were already there. If such conduct does not make you feel cheerful, nothing else on that occasion can.

So, to feel brave, act as if we were brave, use all of our will to that end, and a courage-fit will very likely replace the fit of fear.

Remember too that you probably feel worse than you look. Very few speakers actually look nervous and more than likely your audience is rooting for you. Most audiences are not hostile and generally respond in a friendly way toward speakers.

Your fellow students all will have their turns speaking to the class so they are likely to be compassionate for soon, they will be in your shoes.

Next, take the advice given by Dr. Norman Vincent Peale in his best-selling book, *The Power of Positive Thinking*. **THINK POSITIVELY.** Positive thinking and confident behavior will improve your speech performance. Today's Olympic athletes are counseled by sports psychologists to visualize themselves as performing exactly as they would hope to perform. That is, they are told to meditate and see themselves as being successful. You too can do the same thing. See and hear yourself standing before an audience delivering the best speech of which you are capable. Talk to yourself, tell yourself you can do the job. It works, for, as we come to learn more about ourselves as human beings, we are learning that there is a direct relationship between our self-images and what we are able to do. In many ways, we are the products of our own minds.

Finally, we know that physical exercise is an effective way to decrease the extra adrenalin which contributes to stress and anxiety attacks. Exercise acts as a release for nervous energy, helps ''clear the head'' and re-establishes your equilibrium. Students who do exercise regularly usually deal better with stress than those who don't. Ideally, some kind of physical exercise shortly *before* you give a speech will lower the effects of anxiety. Any type of aerobic exercise will do (walking, jogging, swimming, biking) as long as it gets your heart and lungs working hard.

Remember your reactions from stage fright are only *seemingly* acute. You are not losing control but responding naturally to stress. Speech anxiety may be the biggest obstacle to speaking effectiveness, but through understanding, applying some of the above techniques, your teacher's insights, and gradual exposure, you can overcome it. If you give yourself the chance, you just may end up loving public speaking.

Unlike the written word that can be studied and dissected, reread and even redone, the speech is a once and only interaction. It is truly a "one-shot deal." It comes to the audience quickly, and is normally over in a short period of time. It is estimated that the average rate of delivery for most speakers is 185 wpm and if most people don't listen well, then much of the subject matter will be forgotten or maybe even ignored. Only the most prepared and rehearsed speakers will engage, capture, and sustain an audience's interest. Therefore, we should approach speech preparation with a strategy that is both organized and efficient.

PREPARING A SPEECH

**Topic
Selection,
Research, and
Purpose**

It is true that in some formal speaking situations, you may be asked to speak on a specific subject. More often than not however, you will have to begin your speech preparation by selecting a topic. This first step is crucial to the success of the entire speech process; everything that follows rests on how well you pick a subject. Here are five suggestions to get you started on the right track:

Point 1: Use intrapersonal communication to decide on a topic. Go through your "memory banks" and reflect on those topics that you find interesting. What are your likes and dislikes? What are your hobbies or avocational interests? On what subjects do you normally speak well? What is your field of expertise? Select subjects you find stimulating and then pick a topic you can "believe" in and "sell." Your audience will sense if you are not personally interested. *You can only excite an audience if you are genuinely involved in your subject matter.*

Point 2: Complete an audience analysis to help you decide on a topic. Once you have reflected on your interests and strengths, you should do the same for your audience. Too many speakers make erroneous assumptions about their audiences and wonder why their speeches fail. A little "homework" or research on your audience will reveal important factors to consider as you develop your ideas. In many college speech classes, you will get to know your audience through speeches of introduction that students will be required to give. Later on, in business, you will want to consider the following demographic factors:

Average age of group
Male-female distribution
Educational level
Economic class
Occupational types

A careful analysis of these and other factors will reveal what subjects are likely to be of interest to the group and which are not. Further, such a study will suggest the values and attitudes that members of the audience are likely to have. This combination of self-inventory and audience analysis will allow you to pick a topic that is suited to both you and the people who will be listening to your speech. Be certain the topic will fit the audience's expectations, the time constraints you have been given, and the occasion for the speech.

Point 3: Once you have chosen a topic, you still need to be certain that sufficient information is readily available on the topic so that you may develop the subject to its fullest extent. Naturally, if you have chosen a real-life personal experience to talk about, your need to obtain information elsewhere will be less. With other subjects you need to recall Cicero's warning to aspiring orators: "No man can be eloquent in a subject he does not understand." Understanding comes from information and information comes from researching a topic. Find out if information is available in your library before finalizing your topic. Check the card catalogs, the *Reader's Guide to Periodical Literature,* encyclopedias, and other reference books. Don't limit your investigation to these sources. Community organizations such as Alcoholics Anonymous, the Samaritans, Planned Parenthood, the Right to Life Movement, and most municipal, state, and federal agencies are often excellent sources of material. Members of college and/or university faculties can also be helpful. The point is that information can be found in many places but, before you continue with your speech preparation, determine if *enough* information is available on your topic.

Point 4: Determine the purpose of your speech. Frequently, when we listen to a speech we have only a vague notion of what the speaker wants us to do with the information. Sometimes we are not even sure what the speech was all about. We usually are not sure of the speech's purpose when the speaker hasn't defined his topic clearly and when he has made no attempt to include a central idea or thesis statement. Include a thesis statement or central idea (sometimes called a controlling concept) in your speech to help the audience focus on your purpose. This will remind you of your reason for speaking and it will help the audience listen and comprehend. Write your purpose in a thesis statement (a single, declarative sentence is easiest) before you begin writing the speech. An example could be that you wish to inform a group about first aid procedures within a factory. You may put that into a thesis statement as follows: "When an emergency strikes, all should follow the first aid procedures I have listed from the Red Cross Handbook." The thesis statement should capture the essence of the concept or information that you are trying to communicate. Include that statement or a close variation in your introductory remarks.

There are other ways of revealing your purpose but the beginning speaker should stick to a simple, clear formula. Always ask yourself: Just what am I trying to communicate to this audience? Am I trying to persuade, to inform, to entertain, or some combination of all three. When your purpose is clear in your mind, it will be clear to the audience as well. With your purpose clear and materials gathered together, you are now ready to structure your speech.

Point 5: Organization is the key to a successful speech. If your speech is not organized, it will make the speech difficult to understand and follow. The listeners will be confused if you jump around in a haphazard way. You can make your speech coherent by dividing it into three parts: Introduction, Body, and Conclusion. Remember that your listeners have no way of sitting down and studying your speech like a book or a letter.

There is no second chance for the listeners. Clear organization helps you develop ideas so that each one is a stepping stone to the next. If you destroy the organization of your speech, you destroy its clarity. If the speech is not clear, meaningful interaction with the audience will not take place.

Introductions 10-15%

Though the introduction of a speech should represent only *10%-15%* of the entire speech, many teachers of speech consider it to be the most important part. They reason that you create that vital first impression during your introduction and predispose your audience to feel positively or negatively toward the rest of what you have to say.

The first words you deliver are crucial. Several things ought to happen at the outset of your speech: you should be setting a tone, making an impression, arousing interest in yourself as a speaker, attracting interest in the topic, developing the boundaries or parameters of the topic (some call this signposting the speech) for the audience, and giving the audience your intentions for the speech. If the audience is not with you at the beginning, they will not be with you at the end. *Work at effective introductions.*

Approaches:

The following approaches are recommended for your introductions. Consider combining some of them when appropriate.

1/ ***Refer to the Audience:*** "It is a pleasure to be addressing such an important organization as the Big Brothers of America. You as Big Brothers, bring love, care, and inspiration and guidance to many fatherless boys. I am honored to speak to you today."

2/ ***Refer to the Occasion:*** "The fourth of July is a historic and important celebration in the history of our nation. It is a time when we are reminded of the roots of our independence, our freedom, and the spirit of our American character. It is a time when we praise all who have gone before us and sacrificed themselves for the glory of our Democratic Republic."

3/ ***Refer to the Subject:*** "My speech today is about that old romantic ritual, the high school prom. My hope is to persuade you that high school proms should be done away with and replaced by an occasion that is safer, much less expensive, more democratic, and far less traumatic."

4/ *Refer to Quote:* "As the German philosopher and poet, Friedrich Nietzsche, once stated: 'He who has a *why* to live for can bear almost any *how.*' It is my pleasure to applaud your inspiration and thank you for showing the world the truth of Nietzsche's remark. As former P.O.W.'s, you have shown us life is worth living, no matter how hard the circumstances may be."

5/ *Use a Startling Statement:* "Have yourself a good long look. Because you are looking at a crazy man. A man who has lost his marbles. A man who needs a straight-jacket. Because according to the standards of American society, I'm crazy!"

6/ *Use a Rhetorical Question:* "Have you ever felt fear? Have you ever panicked? Have you ever felt like 'flipping out?' Have you ever lost control because of anxiety? If you answered yes, you may have a phobia."

7/ *Use Humor:* "Tonight, at your graduation ceremonies, you have asked me to share my wisdom with you. Though that part of my speech will only take a few seconds, I believe I can still inspire you. I reflect on the inspiration my coach gave me when I was pitching in a close baseball game. He said: 'Son, it may seem like a bad spot to be in, but receive hope from this — that even a blind squirrel finds some nuts.'"

Whatever approach or combination of approaches you decide to use, be certain that your introduction connects logically and smoothly to the body of your speech.

The Body of the Speech 70-80%

The Body or the Discussion section of your speech should be *70%-80%* of the whole. The basic problem with many speakers is that they think too much like writers and not enough like speechmakers. Your audience cannot study, reread, or dwell on any one point for an extended period of time. Unlike written information, oral communication is flowing like a river and it cannot be stopped in any one place. There is an old speech saying that states: "Tell them what you are going to tell them, tell them, and then tell them what you told them." If there is any type of communication that needs a little "redundancy," it is speech communication. You must help your audience to retain, and repetition is certainly called for in your speeches.

The organizational set up that you follow should be selected with the audience in mind. Only a few organizational patterns are recommended for the beginning speaker. The following patterns are recommended: Topical Patterns, Sequential Patterns, Causal Patterns, Problem-Solution Patterns.

The Topical Pattern:

Just as the name implies, this is a speech arrangement that is divided according to well-known topics or categories that you can easily classify. For example, you may want to speak on the top three automobile manufacturers in the U.S. You could easily arrange this as follows:

    I. Ford Motor Company
      a. History and Development
      b. Present Day Activity
      c. Future Innovations
   II. General Motors Company
      a. History and Development
      b. Present Day Activity
      c. Future Innovations
  III. Chrysler Motor Company
      a. History and Development
      b. Present Day Activity
      c. Future Innovations

The thing to remember about the *Topical Pattern* is that you can classify almost any speech by using this arrangement. Just break down your subject according to types, kinds, categories, reasons, groups, traits, parts, advantages, disadvantages, etc., and you are using the Topical Pattern.

The Sequential Pattern:

This type of arrangement is based on space and time. Many sources call this "Spatial" arrangement and "Chronological" arrangement. The "Spatial" approach could be used in a discussion of the geography of the New England states. You could arrange your speech by moving in sequence from the State of Maine to the State of Connecticut (North to South). The thing to remember about this sequential pattern is physical space or geographic proximity is used to show relationship and to produce unity. The "Chronological" approach is simply the use of *time* in a systematic way. If you are giving a speech on how to fill out your income tax forms, you can talk about what needs to be done first, and then progress from the next point to another. Or if you were to give a speech on American involvement in Viet Nam, you could begin with the signing of the first treaty with Viet Nam to the eventual collapse of the government. The "Chronological" approach is an excellent one for "how to" speeches or "historic" speeches.

The Causal Pattern:

This type of arrangement shows a relationship between certain factors and what follows them. The causal pattern should be thought of as an arrangement that shows causes and effects. You could show how TV watching produces anti-social behavior in children and adolescents. You could cite increases in violent crime and threatening behavior after "gang" movies were shown on major networks in large cities.

The Problem-Solution Pattern:

This is an effective arrangement when you are proposing a change or suggesting an alternative to a present-day problem. If you were to give a speech on drug addiction, and then make suggestions for answers to the problem, this type of pattern would be ideal. You could set up the speech easily by showing the seriousness of the problem and then conclude your speech by making recommendations for the solution.

Whatever pattern you decide to use, always remember that your goal is communication. Many speakers lose their audiences because they never make organizational selections based on the capability of their listeners. Always subscribe to the principles of unity, coherence, and emphasis. Make sure every part of the speech fits together well. Don't confuse the audience by jumping around, bringing in extraneous information, or not elaborating on statements made. Remember you need a plan that works for you and your audience. Your plan should give you a singleness of purpose: one that shows your speech is *unified*. Also allow your audience to see the continuity, the consistency, and direction of your speech. *Coherence* means the fitting together of the thoughts you utter. It should not be a random selection of material and supporting information. Again you need to be unified, and continual in the production of your thesis. The last thing to remember is to use *emphasis* in your organization. You should give prominence to some ideas and subordination to other ideas. You can achieve emphasis by using 1/ proportion — the length of time you devote to an idea; 2/ repetition — the number of times you repeat your ideas in either the same way or a slightly different way; and 3/ position — the location of your ideas in the speech. The last type of emphasis, position, is largely a psychological matter. You have to decide where the best position for an idea is in your speech.

Conclusions
10-15%

Many untrained speakers don't know how to disengage themselves from the audience. They either hem and haw, ramble on and on without knowing where to stop or stop too abruptly as if they had to jam on the brakes at a light which had suddenly turned red. In so doing, they spoil the last opportunity they have to make a desired impact on the audience. They are ignoring that old truism of communication theory: "That which is said first is usually the attracting or arousing thing; that which is said last is usually the thing that is most remembered, most retained." Your conclusion should be remembered as the climax of your speech. It should be remembered as the most memorable part of your speech. It is the last thing the audience will hear. A good conclusion should do the following: 1/ let the audience know you are ending (use concluding words like *so, thus, finally, to conclude, to sum up, my final remarks, let me finish by restating my thesis, therefore,* and the like); 2/ restate what you want them to understand about your topic; 3/ leave a final impression, 4/ and disengage yourself from the audience in a meaningful way. Like any good business letter or any good musical piece, your conclusion should be looked upon as a closure or a finale. Make your last few words important words. Don't forget to signal your conclusion to the audience by using the appropriate words.

Many of the ways you can introduce a speech can also be used for concluding a speech. You have to decide what the best way is for your purpose.

Select the most appropriate approach below. Decide on your purpose and use the following effective method. You may want to combine approaches.

Approaches:

> *1/ **Refer to the Audience:*** "So, tonight, as I leave this meeting, I will receive strength from the knowledge that all of you here will not abandon our cause. You are the type of people who have ideals and pursue them, and I am encouraged in my efforts because you stick to the fight when you're hardest hit."

2/ Refer to the Occasion: "Finally, as we reflect on this Veterans' Day, let us recall the many men and women who have served this Country well. Let us remember their sacrifices, so that we today, can truly say we are free Americans."

3/ Refer to the Subject: "My speech this afternoon has focused on the need for dialogue between management and labor. All management personnel should institute the four main steps of the dialogue process in their respective departments. Copies of my speech will be distributed via you mail boxes so as to help you in this crucial process."

4/ Refer to a Quote: "As I conclude tonight, I recall the words of the great New England poet, Robert Frost: 'The woods are lovely, dark and deep, but I have promises to keep, and miles to go before I sleep, and miles to go before I sleep."

5/ Refer to a Story or Illustration: "Let me end by sharing with you a brief story about a businessman who had a dream, and turned that dream into a multi-million dollar enterprise which today is IBM."

6/ Refer to a Rhetorical Question: "So, is it not better for us to be in full discussion with management, than to close down negotiations and go on strike?"

7/ Issue an Appeal or Challenge the Audience to Action: "Since the next few months are critical to our company, I ask all of you to hold the line on your budgets. If we can do that, we may be able to forego the expected layoffs, and get all of our employees back to work."

8/ Summarize Your Main Points: "Each person is asked to follow the steps I have outlined for the computer's use. To highlight the main points again, I recommend the following:"

Outlining the Speech

Once you have developed an organizational structure for your speech in rough notes, you need to formulate a more specific outline of your material. At this stage, you are much like a builder who has sketched a general design of a house he plans to build. Next, he must draw up a specific blueprint so that he may move to the construction phase. Your blueprint is an outline which lists in order the specific steps you plan to take in your speech. Once the outline is completed, you will be ready to write the speech. Following is a format that you can use for all your speeches with the exception of the impromptu speech discussed later.

Title of Speech: _____

Purpose of Speech: _____

Time of Speech: _____

Type of Audience: _____

I. INTRODUCTION
    A. Use one or a combination of suggested approaches.
    B. Preview the speech.
        1. Set the tone.
        2. Give your thesis or main idea. Make sure your focus is clear.
        3. Give your intentions for the topic and set the parameters of your speech.
        4. Arouse interest in yourself as a speaker.
        5. Arouse interest in your subject.

II. THE BODY OR DISCUSSION AREA
    A. Support of your thesis.
    B. Use the most appropriate pattern of organization.
    C. Elaborate on main points.
        1. Give major ideas larger treatment.
        2. Divide speech to accent those major ideas.
        3. Subordinate minor or lesser ideas.
        4. Develop ideas well enough for the comprehension level of your audience.
        5. Check your logic for these points:
            a. Unity and Continuity
            b. Coherence
            c. Emphasis
        6. Never make a statement without considering the support you will give it. If an idea is not generally agreed upon knowledge, then consider elaborating and developing that idea more fully. (Again, the capability of your audience has a lot to say about the development of an idea.)

7. Finally, when you check your discussion area, ask yourself if you fulfilled the expectations and intentions of your Introduction. Make sure you do what you told the audience you were going to do.

III. CONCLUSION

A. Use one or more of the suggested approaches.

B. Sum up, review, or refocus the main areas of the speech. Make sure the "essence" or "reason to be" is now entirely clear. By this time your thesis should be self-evident. A reminder of that position can help your audience to retain.

C. Make the last few words of your speech appropriate for your audience.

D. Disengage yourself positively from your audience. Know exactly how you are going to conclude and *never be indecisive*. Those last few moments the audience will be making their final assessment about you. Once you have concluded, thank the audience for their attention, and then sit down.

The actual flow of the outline should look like this:

Your Name: __Paul Smith__

Title of Speech: __"A MAN FOR ALL SEASONS"__

Purpose of Speech: __TO REINFORCE THE HIGH OPINION OF THE__

__AUDIENCE FOR P.O.W. ADMIRAL STOCKDALE__

Time of Speech: __10 MINUTES__

Type of Audience: __MILITARY PERSONNEL AND THEIR FAMILIES__

I. INTRODUCTION

A. Refer to the Audience and the occasion.

B. Use "Factors of Attention": Familiarity, Reality, and Proximity.

C. Preview.

II. THE BODY OF THE SPEECH

A. Reasons for praising Admiral Stockdale.

B. Use of the "Chronological" Sequential Pattern.

C. Discussion of Admiral Stockdale's entrance into the military to his role in Viet Nam and his eventual detention in North Viet Nam as a P.O.W.

        D. Examples and Illustrations of his unusual bravery and
          courage.
        E. Use of Testimonial by fellow P.O.W.

III. CONCLUSION
        A. Refer to another illustration; refer to the Audience;
          end with a Climax.
        B. Use a Quote from the President of the United States
          about Admiral Stockdale and all P.O.W.'s and then
          disengage yourself from the audience.
        C. Ask for applause from audience. (More than likely
          they would already be applauding Admiral Stock-
          dale.)

WRITING THE SPEECH AND USING VISUAL AIDS

The outline of the speech has given you the skeletal structure which has to be filled in with the words, sentences, and paragraphs of your choice. Choose your words carefully, selecting ones that are above all else clear and unambiguous. Use sentences and paragraphs to break your subject down into as many smaller parts as possible and start with the simpler parts and progress to the more difficult.

Write the speech as you would like to deliver it even though, in most situations, it is unlikely that you will give it exactly as you have written it. Pay close attention to the wording and phrasing of your introduction and conclusion as both are crucial to overall success. Keep your audience in mind when choosing vocabulary; if members of your audience are unfamiliar with words that you use, not only will understanding be lost but there just might be some resentment stirred up as well.

During this stage of preparation, you may also decide that visual aids would be a helpful supplement. Before you do, consider the advice of Lee Pitre and Larry Smeltzer in an article entitled ''Graphic Reinforcement for an Oral Presentation'' published in the *ABCA Bulletin* in December 1982:

> A picture is worth a thousand words ... if it supports rather than distracts from the message, if it accurately conveys the message, if it can be seen by everyone in the audience, and if it is easily interpreted by the audience. A picture is worth a thousand words when the correct visual technique is used and it is well designed.

Pitre and Smeltzer go on to say that any visual aid must meet three criteria: 1/ visibility, 2/ clarity, 3/ simplicity. To meet these criteria, the number of words used on charts should be few, visual aids should be colorful, and graphs or charts should be simple and unified.[1]

Also, be sure that your graphics are suited to the place where you are speaking. Don't assume there will be chalk, charts, projectors, or electrical outlets at your disposal. Check ahead of time to be certain the place is suitable and whatever equipment is needed will be there. (See Table I.)

Table I
VISUAL AIDS

Equipment	Audience Size	Advantages	Disadvantages
Flip Charts	Depending on size of chart, up to 30.	Inexpensive, easy to use, no protection required.	Limited audience size, difficult to carry around.
Desk Charts	Approximately 5.	Like flip chart, but may be placed on desk. Allows you to remain at desk. Easy to handle.	Limited audience size
Blackboard	Up to 30.	Convenient, no planning required.	Unprofessional appearance, can't take advantage of colors or detailed diagrams.
Overhead Projector	Up to 45.	Best for materials requiring extensive discussion. Inexpensive. Allows you to face the group.	A projector and screen are required. Room needs to be shaped for ease in viewing the screen. Reduced lights is encouraged.
35mm Slides	Limited only by size of room and screen size.	Give image of professionalism and preparation.	Costly and time-consuming to produce. Room must be darkened. Screen and projector must be available.

(from "Graphic Reinforcement for an Oral Presentation" by Lee Pitre and Larry Smeltzer — *ABCA Bulletin,* December 1982)

REHEARSING THE SPEECH

After you have written out the speech in its entirety, you need to begin to reread it. At the same time as you are committing much of what you have written to memory, you are practicing or rehearsing. Don't worry about memorizing the speech word for word; just get down the essence of what you have written in the order that you wish to deliver it.

Rehearsal may be done in a number of different ways:

- Speak it aloud while alone in an office or automobile.

- Deliver the speech to a friend or family member who will not be too critical nor too complimentary in their review.

- Use any machines you have (tape recorder or videotaping unit) and play it back alone and in the company of a few critics. If you can't find anyone to practice in front of, at least use a mirror and check your facial expression, and posture to see if your speech is "together." Once everything is together, you are ready to deliver the speech. Remember, the greater the preparation, the lesser the speech anxiety.

FOUR TYPES OF DELIVERY

All speeches and the situations in which they are given are not the same. Before we proceed further to discuss specific kinds of speeches, we need to study the four methods of delivery for speech makers.

The first method of delivery is the *Extemporaneous Speech.* The extemporaneous speech is one that is planned and rehearsed, uses a brief speaking outline or notes, and yet possesses an air or degree of spontaneity. It is the type of delivery that your teacher will require most of you to use in your classroom speaking assignments. It gives you freedom to make adjustments as you deliver your speech and at the same time you have your speaking outline or "roadmap" before you so you know what must be covered. The extemporaneous method can be used in all types of business settings. A major advantage of the extemporaneous speech is the flexibility you possess. You are not locked into a script, you are freer to look at your audience, you are able to make audience adaptations quickly, and you have the "safety" of your notes before you. If you are going to speak to groups in your career, the extemporaneous approach is highly recommended.

The second method of delivery is the *Impromptu Speech.* Unlike the extemporaneous speech, the impromptu is not prepared. It is literally "off the top of your head." The impromptu is thinking on your feet and speaking well enough to make your audience take notice. This type of speech is given all the time. You may be asked to say a few words in a meeting without any preparation or forewarning. You could deliver this type of speech at a PTA gathering or at a town budget meeting. The impromptu speaker must quickly assess the situation and come across as reasonable and knowledgeable. Although you have very little time for preparation, you should try to use the few moments that you have to structure your thoughts for a fluid delivery. The impromptu speech is a difficult method of delivery and should not be your standard approach to speeches. Even Mark Twain said it took him "at least three weeks to prepare a good impromptu speech!" If you must speak impromptu, you should use those things that have been addressed before your speech to maintain continuity between your topic and the others. You should try to relate to those people who have spoken before you and remember that you cannot speak well for long without preparation. Get to the point and offer the floor to another. If you are the first to speak or if you are wondering how to focus your speech quickly, address the "journalistic questions" — who? what? when? where? why? and how? If these points are clear, more than likely your audience will be able to comprehend your message. There is a tendency in impromptu speaking to be vague because of the lack of preparation and the short time to speak. A good impromptu speaker can be a valuable asset in an organization. However, it is not recommended that you depend on your ability to "ad lib" to deliver. Preparation is always preferred.

The third method of delivery is the *Manuscript Speech.* This method is just as the name implies. You use a manuscript or written text and read the speech to your audience. This is the type of speech that many top executives deliver because they have speech writers prepare their talks. The writer will usually type in large print that is spread out across the page (5-9 words per line), and spaced out with three to four lines between each sentence. The manuscript speech is also used in situations where a speaker's information will be recorded verbatim. This is done frequently in Congressional proceedings or in courtroom situations. The manuscript speech can be used effectively in highly emotional settings, such as funerals. The eulogy speech can be a very emotional experience and having the script with you is a good idea. Senator Edward M. Kennedy used a manuscript when delivering the eulogy of his brother, the late Senator Robert F. Kennedy, at St. Patrick's Cathedral. The President and many national and state officials will use a manuscript when they address the press. Sometimes they give the press corps copies before they deliver it publicly so they can prepare their reports, questions, and analyses. This method has been used in most of the recent Presidential inaugural addresses.

Any business person can use this approach to speaking and even hire a speech writer if their budget allows. But there is a tendency to "read" the speech and not really "deliver" it. It is easy to not notice the audience and to make no eye contact. If someone else has written it for you, it may sound artificial and may not be written in your "style." There is also the problem of being unfamiliar with the content which could hinder your credibility if questions were to arise. Further, if you are locked into a script, there is little room for audience adaptation. Still, for the beginning speaker in a class such as yours, using the manuscript method for your first few efforts may help you overcome some of the initial problems of stage fright. Your teacher can help you decide which method to select for the first few assignments.

The last method of delivery is the *Memorized Speech.* Many beginning speakers believe if they memorize their speeches, they will have no problems. There is nothing further from the truth. Usually you are setting yourself up for forgetting the speech. If you lose your "train of thought," you may panic and not be able to continue. Unless you are a practiced speaker, like an actor or actress, or perhaps a tour guide or someone who gives the same talk over and over to groups, the memorized speech is not recommended. The business speaker would do better to concentrate on the extemporaneous or manuscript method of delivery. If you have a choice, prefer the extemporaneous speech. It gives you the most freedom to speak.

SPEECH DELIVERY

Deliver your speech in a forceful, dynamic way. Use all your skills, verbal and nonverbal, to enthusiastically deliver your message. The best advice we can give you on delivery is to consider the four channels you have at your disposal to prepare. Those channels are: 1/ *Verbal* — it carries the words we use; 2/ *Visual* it transmits the gestures, facial expressions, bodily movements, posture, and the entire nonverbal presence of the speaker; 3/ *Pictorial* — it carries any visual aids you may use. Aids like pictures, graphs, charts, handouts, models, films, slides, printed information, and the like. 4/ *Aural* — This is also termed the paralinguistic medium — it carries the tone of voice, variations in pitch and loudness, resonance, inflection, force, duration, intensity, and the like. Remember that vocal modulation can improve the reception of your message. *Remember, it is not only what you say, but how you say it that counts!*

Following is a typical critique sheet that is used in college classrooms to evaluate a speech *after* it has been given. Look at it beforehand so that you are reminded of the things you need to do.

Speech Evaluation

*SPEAKER*_____ *SUBJECT OF TALK*_____

DATE _____ *EVALUATED BY* _____

	Poor	*Very Weak*	*Weak*	*Fair*	*Adequate*	*Good*	*Very Good*	*Excellent*	*Superior*
	1	2	3	4	5	6	7	8	9
1. Introduction									
2. Clarity of purpose									
3. Choice of words									
4. Bodily action-gesture-posture									
5. Eye contact and facial expression									
6. Vocal expression									
7. Desire to be understood									
8. Poise and self-control									
9. Adapting material to audience									
10. Organization of material									
11. Conclusion									

Model Speech **Public Speaking and Other Coronary Threats**
The Value of Self Improvement

Max D. Isaacson, Vice President, Administration, Macmillan Oil
Delivered to Speechcraft Students at Des Moines City Hall,
Des Moines, Iowa, February 1, 1980

In my job and at other functions, quite often I'm called on to speak and my wife says that I get up so often that I'm living proof of the old adage that hot air always rises. But I have something a little more substantial than hot air to talk about today.

I'm glad you are here because that tells me you've had the dedication and the interest in this important Speechcraft course. I can tell you from personal experience that the ability to express oneself well in public is certainly valuable in my business and in every walk of life that I know of.

In addition to my interest in public speaking, I'm happy to be here for another reason. Since I'm on the staff of an oil company, I'm happy to be invited anywhere where there is a cordial reception ... that's a pleasant accomplishment.

Speaking of accomplishments, your chairman asked me to speak on "Accomplishments Through Speechcraft." A more appropriate title might be: *"PUBLIC SPEAKING AND OTHER CORONARY THREATS!"* because in public speaking, many are called but few want to get up. You know and I know that it can be scary indeed to get up to address a group. But listen to these statements.

Daniel Webster said:

"If all my possessions were taken from me with one exception, I would choose to keep the power of speech, for by it I would soon regain all the rest (of my possessions)."

Sigmund Freud observed:

"Words call forth emotions and are universally the means by which we influence our fellow creatures ... by words, one of us can give to another the greatest happiness or bring about utter despair."

The eminent Dale Carnegie said:

"Every activity of our lives is communication of a sort, but it is through speech that man asserts his distinctiveness ... that he best expresses his own individuality, his essence."

Someone else has observed, and I certainly agree, that "self-confidence has always been the first secret of success." Of the known phobias — and there is a long list of them — the fear of public speaking consistently ranks at the top in public surveys. It's even more feared than death. But why should intelligent people fear public speaking?

Most of us have at least average intelligence and when we look around us — at co-workers, bosses, politicians — we know that our level of knowledge is as great or greater than theirs, but the thing that so often separates us is our inability to feel confident when expressing ourselves ... we fear to speak up.

It's true that we make ourselves vulnerable when we speak up ... vulnerable to criticism. It's usually easier and more comfortable to stay out of the spotlight and to languish in the comfort of the non-speaker's role, to avoid the risk of feeling inferior.

But I've always been fond of quoting Eleanor Roosevelt on the subject of self-confidence and it was she who said: "No one can make you feel inferior without your consent." Think about that for a moment. "No one can make you feel inferior without your consent." Isn't that a remarkable statement?

And here are some remarkable figures to prove that man is his own worst enemy. *MORE PERSONS KILL THEMSELVES EACH YEAR THAN MURDER OTHERS.* There are 25,000 suicides annually in the U.S. and 18,000 homicides. Suicide is the severest form of self-hatred. But a milder form of self-hatred is the inferiority complex many of us secretly harbor.

One of my kids recently told me a riddle. He said, "Dad, do you know what the largest room in the world is?" "The largest room ...?" I replied that I did not. He answered, *"THE ROOM FOR IMPROVEMENT!"* That's why I believe in Speechcraft, because it's a valuable means for improvement. It offers what most of us need to become better public speakers.

Isn't it incredible that there is so little emphasis throughout our educational and business training on this needed skill of oral communication? I've found that in high school, college, military service, graduate school and in business, any emphasis on oral communication *HAS BEEN CONSPICUOUS BY ITS ABSENCE.* And yet, you and I communicate orally more than in any other way when dealing with people.

Some time ago I attended a conference whose main speaker was a nationally-known management expert and he said that we are not in the oil business, the insurance business, the government service business, the manufacturing business ... rather *WE ARE IN THE PEOPLE BUSINESS!* It behooves us to do whatever we can to improve our communications among people in all walks of life in order to improve human relations.

Where will you go from here? What will you do with the valuable experience you've gained at these Speechcraft sessions? Unfortunately, most persons stop their training after the formal Speechcraft course has ended. They apparently are satisfied with their progress or don't want to make the effort to continue. But can you imagine a pianist stopping after 10 lessons and saying, "I've arrived — and I'm now accomplished!"? Public speaking takes on-going practice so I would encourage you to stick with it through regular Toastmaster training.

I'm convinced you'll do better on the job, in your community organizations and in your house of worship. One of my biggest thrills was that of becoming a certified lay speaker in the United Methodist Church — just one of the many ways that experience in public speaking can be applied for personal fulfillment and self-realization.

Let me close with a thought that I've shared with graduating high school seniors and other groups concerning the value of self-improvement. It goes like this:

> God said, "Build a better world,"
> And I said, "How?"
> The world is such a cold, dark place and so complicated now
> And I so young and useless, there's nothing I can do,
> But God in all his wisdom said, "Just build a better you."

Reprinted by permission of "Vital Speeches of the Day."

6 ▌▌▌

FOUR TYPES OF SPEECHES FOR CLASSROOM PRACTICE

In the previous section you learned the generally accepted theory relating to public speaking. Now it is time to apply that theory to classroom practice. Your instructor will guide you in the way that he or she prefers. Topics will either be assigned or you will be able to choose your own. What follows is a *suggested* sequence of speeches which has worked well in college classrooms for a long time. Study the requirements for each type of speech, follow the ideas previously suggested, and the results that follow will surprise even the most inexperienced student. Relax. Enjoy yourself and remember that you are acquiring a skill that will be a major asset in your future careers.

The Speech of Self-Introduction

It is very often a pattern in communications skills classes that the first speech you will be expected to give is one in which you introduce yourself to other members of the class. There are three major advantages to beginning this way: first, the self-introductory speech serves as an excellent "ice breaker," allowing each speaker the opportunity to experience and overcome "speech anxiety" in a situation where the content of the speech is not a problem to prepare. Second, each class member gets to know the other people in the class. The result is that a clear picture of the audience emerges. This is useful when preparing future speeches. The third benefit is that the self-introductory speech is precisely what you will have to do, in one form or another, shortly after you begin your business career.

Format:

This first speech should be brief (1-3 minutes). Provide the basic biographical information the audience will need such as name, age, where you are from, what year you are in, and what major course you are or will be studying. Once the facts are established, you might consider explaining how you chose the college you are attending and your long-term career ambitions. As your speech progresses, give the audience a glimpse of your personal self. Share with them some of your likes and dislikes, how you spend your leisure time, and the things you consider interesting and entertaining. Finally, as with any speech, thank the audience for their attention and move slowly back to your seat.

**Model Speech
Self-
Introduction**

Good Afternoon. My name is Mary Gorham. I am twenty years old and my home town is Mamaroneck, New York, which is a village about twenty miles outside of New York City in Westchester County. Mamaroneck is located on the Long Island Sound and is a suburban community from which many residents commute daily by train to their work in New York.

My major is in Data Processing and I chose Central College because of the up-to-date curriculum it offered and the modern equipment that is available for student use. After graduation, my hope is to get a job with a progressive corporation that has a need for people with my training. Eventually, I plan to go to graduate school in the evenings or on weekends.

One of the major problems I know I will have to face is to balance my career aspirations with my desire to marry and have children. I hope I will be able to sort out my feelings on this question while I am here in college.

In the meantime, when I am not studying, I enjoy jogging and playing tennis. Keeping physically fit is important to me as I seem to work better and I am happier when I feel healthy. However, with all those good intentions, I also enjoy parties, concerts, and being with groups of my peers.

My objective in this class is to learn to communicate more effectively and, in particular, to get over my nervousness so that I can speak comfortably to groups.

Thank you for listening to me. I appreciate your attention.

84

Follow your instructor's directions for using this outline.

Outline of Speech

Name:_____

Title of Speech: _____

Purpose of Speech: _____

Type of Audience: _____

Time of Speech: _____

I. INTRODUCTION

    A.

        1.

        2.

    B.

        1.

        2.

    C.

        1.

        2.

II. BODY OF SPEECH

    A.

        1.

        2.

    B.

        1.

        2.

C.

    1.

    2.

D.

    1.

    2.

III. CONCLUSION

A.

    1.

    2.

B.

    1.

    2.

C.

    1.

    2.

D.

    1.

    2.

**The
Informative
Speech**

The next type of speech to address is the informative speech. Just as the title implies, the purpose of this speech is to pass on information. The key point here is to try to pick a topic that will be new to the audience, either partially or in its entirety. Find something in your preparation and research that is fresh or interesting. Avoid the "old" topics that the audience has heard before unless you can bring new insights to them. The point is this: don't choose a topic that is stale.

If your speech is to be truly informative, it also must be impartial, accurate, and complete. A common problem for student speakers is that their informative speeches often turn out to be persuasive. This can be avoided if you remind yourself that your purpose is to gain understanding among your listeners, not to convince them of your own point-of-view.

Audience analysis is crucial to the success of informative speeches. Tailor your material to your listeners. For example, if you are explaining how stress can be overcome by a regular exercise program, you might relate the material to the times when students experience the most stress which, for most students, is exam time. A good informative speech is personally valuable or useful for the audience. Ideally the audience should have a stake in the information given. Instead of giving a speech on meditation, perhaps you could focus it like this: "Meditation: 15 minutes every day will improve your grades!"

Be sure your information is tightly organized. The longer a speech, the more difficult it is to follow. You should make every attempt to see that all parts are clear and that transitions from Introductions to Conclusions are explicit. Keep in mind the old speech adage: Tell them what you are going to tell them *(Introduction)*; tell them *(Body and Discussion)*; and then tell them what you have told them *(Conclusion)*.

> *Introduction:* Have you ever seen someone die? Did you ever feel helpless in an emergency? Would you like to be prepared? Today I will show you the steps to follow when you see an accident or come upon a person who needs emergency aid.
> *Body:* (I will demonstrate on this Red Cross model.) First check the person for a pulse or feel just under his nose to see if he is breathing.
> *Conclusion:* As I stated previously, you don't have to feel helpless in an emergency. Again, the steps that we focused on today are: First . . .

Format:

The time allotted for informative speeches will vary with each class and each instructor. Five to ten minutes is a reasonable time period and is dependent on your topic. Time yourself when you rehearse your speech and, then, adjust your material and rate of presentation to fit the suggested time framework.

Remember your task is to inform. You may do this by a simple oral explanation or by "demonstrating" a skill or technique that requires physical movement. A speech on nutrition that shows the audience how to prepare vegetarian and fruit breakfasts for improved emotional and physical health is an example of a demonstration that is informative. Both types (oral or demonstration) can be enhanced by the use of graphics or audio-visuals as discussed earlier.

This is your first major speech. Accept the challenge to do it well. Once you develop the skill to pass on information clearly in an interesting manner, you will be able to call on that skill again and again throughout your career.

Model Speech
Informative

How the Heart Works
Benjamin F. Edwards II

Do you realize, as you are sitting here, that the heart of each of you is beating 70 times per minute, 4,200 times per hour, and over 100,000 times every day? And that, although each time it beats, only this much blood is squeezed out, *(Here, 65cc. of red liquid is poured into a common drinking glass, to bring in the familiar.)* your heart pumps over 6,000 quarts of blood every day, and in 19 days, it would pump enough blood to fill this whole room.

But what makes your heart beat? Why is it that it can beat year in and year out without tiring? What will speed it up, or slow it down? In the next five minutes I will try to answer these questions for you. In other words, I'm going to tell you how the heart works. *(Please note in the following discussion each structure is pointed to on the chart as it is mentioned.)*

First, I would like to give you a brief description of the anatomy of the heart. Here is a picture of the heart as it really looks. As you can see, it is about the size of my fist. Here *(pointing to chart)* is the heart in diagram form. Think of this heart as being my heart. In other words, as I face you, the upper right hand corner of this heart corresponds to the upper right hand corner of my heart, the lower left hand corner of this heart, with the lower left hand corner of my heart, and so on.

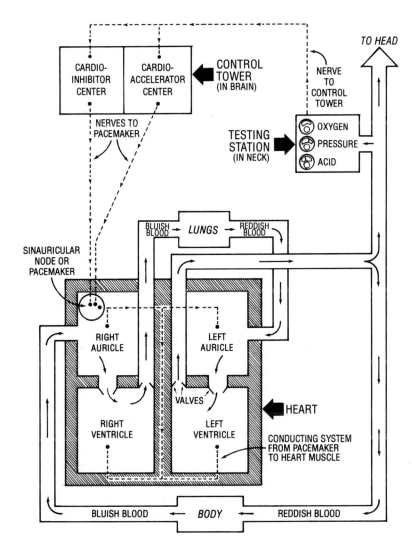

Now, I want you to think of your heart as being a two-story, four-room house. The two upstairs rooms are known as "auricles." They receive the blood. The two downstairs rooms are known as "ventricles." They pump the blood. To reiterate then, the auricles are receiving stations, the ventricles are pumping stations.

But what makes the heart beat? I want you to compare this sinauricular node, or pacemaker of the heart, to a coxswain. Just as he sits in the back of a shell yelling "stroke, stroke," so does this pacemaker sit in the upper right-hand room, that is the right auricle, and yell "stroke" to the heart. This pacemaker does not actually yell, of course, but it sends out impulses over this conducting system which cause the heart muscle to contract every eight tenths of a second.

The impulse reaches the auricles first and they contract for one tenth of a second, and then rest for seven tenths of a second. Then the impulse reaches the ventricles, causing them to contract immediately after the auricles for three tenths of a second and rest for five tenths of a second. Now you can see why the heart can beat indefinitely. Each cycle lasts eight tenths of a second, and out of this eight tenths, the auricles are resting seven tenths and the ventricles are resting five tenths.

By now you should be able to understand, in general, how the blood circulates. As you can see, the heart is really two different pumps, each consisting of an auricle and a ventricle. Well, the blood returns from the body, here, and enters the right auricle. This blood is bluish, since it has given up its oxygen to the body. From the right auricle it goes to the right ventricle *(all the time pointing to the chart)* and then out this way to the lungs. In the lungs it picks up oxygen, then goes back through the left auricle, left ventricle and back to the body. Get that now? Body, right heart, lungs, left heart, and back to the body.

But what governs the speed of the heart? A normal adult heart beats 70 times per minute, an athlete's heart 40 times per minute, and a child's 125 times per minute. This control tower in your brain is responsible for the speed of your heart. It consists of a cardioinhibitor and a cardioaccelerator center. The cardioinhibitor center sends impulses down this nerve to the coxswain or pacemaker and tells him to send out less impulses and thus make the heart go slower. In an opposite manner, the cardioaccelerator center sends impulses down this nerve and tells the pacemaker to speed up the heart.

However, although this control tower governs the speed of your heart, it in turn receives messages from this testing station which is located in the carotid artery in your neck. The carotid artery is the large blood vessel which carries blood to your head. In this testing station, or carotid sinus as we call it, are cells which are sensitive to changes in pressure, acidity, and oxygen content of your blood. Let me illustrate.

For instance, if the amount of oxygen in your blood tests too low, you will faint immediately, because your brain is not getting enough oxygen. This is prevented by the cells in the testing station which are sensitive to changes in the oxygen content of your blood. They send messages along this nerve, telling the cardioaccelerator center to work harder and the cardioinhibitor center to let up. The cardioaccelerator center then sends messages down this nerve, as I have explained. The heart goes faster, pumping more blood through the lungs where it, that is, the blood, picks up more oxygen, and the oxygen content of your blood is raised.

In a similar manner, pressure-sensitive cells in your testing station make the heart, when necessary, go faster, thus raising your blood pressure, or slower, thus lowering the blood pressure. Since too high blood pressure might result in a cerebral hemorrhage, or too low blood pressure might result in fainting, you can see that your testing station maintains an optimum pressure between these two extremes.

Again, in much the same manner, acid-sensitive cells cause your heart to beat faster when there is more acid in your blood from exercise.

Thus you can see that your heart is constantly under various influences attempting either to speed it up or slow it down. At one time, one of these influences may predominate, at another time, some other influence may predominate. Also you should now be able to understand why your heart can beat day in and day out, since, as I have explained, the auricles rest seven eighths of each cycle and the ventricles rest five eighths.

In conclusion, there are three things I would like you to remember. One, auricles receive blood. Two, ventricles pump blood. Three, blood goes from the body to the right side of the heart, to the lungs, to the left side, to the body again. Body, right side, lungs, left side, body. If you can't remember even these three points, please remember that the heart is *NOT* a one-chambered organ, and it does not look like the ones you see on valentines.

Follow your instructor's directions for using this outline.

Outline of Speech

*Name:*_____

Title of Speech: _____

Purpose of Speech: _____

Type of Audience: _____

Time of Speech: _____

I. INTRODUCTION

    A.

        1.

        2.

    B.

        1.

        2.

    C.

        1.

        2.

II. BODY OF SPEECH

    A.

        1.

        2.

    B.

        1.

        2.

      C.

         1.

         2.

      D.

         1.

         2.

III. CONCLUSION

      A.

         1.

         2.

      B.

         1.

         2.

      C.

         1.

         2.

      D.

         1.

         2.

The Personal Experience Speech

The personal experience speech could be looked upon as a logical continuation of the self-introduction speech. You are asked to reveal to your audience an experience that had an impact on your life. Ideally, the impact should be significant enough for you to have learned a lesson and for the other members of the class to gather something from your experience.

You are giving part of yourself to your audience. Whether or not you realize it, the whole speech communication process is a giving of yourself to members of your audience. Your credibility will improve with the extent of your sincerity; to reveal yourself, honestly, will actually increase the effect of your message. *Remember,* the audience can tell a "phony" and not being *you* will only increase your anxiety.

Select an experience that is fresh in your mind or that you can recollect well. Perhaps you have learned things from travel, attending schools, playing sports, recovering from an accident, developing a hobby, and the like. Don't think that your life is uneventful or uninteresting. There are many experiences we have all been through with which others could empathize and gather insight, if you search your memory.

Format:

You should keep the personal experience brief. It is recommended that you keep it under five minutes. Since you are familiar with the experience, you will not have to do any research. Prepare the speech like any other speech. Make sure you have a specific thesis in mind and that your audience will understand explicitly your purpose for sharing. A brief outline is sufficient for this effort. Don't try to memorize your speech. Use your outline or brief notes to remind you of the chronological sequence of the events of your story. Try to keep your language informal but not overly conversational.

The important thing to remember, again, is your audience. If you have a good idea about their various interests, hobbies, likes and dislikes, you should have a good understanding of how to compose the speech (You have learned these types of things by listening to the self-introduction speeches of your classmates.) Select a topic that is worthwhile enough to instruct or entertain the audience. As you prepare this speech, ask yourself: "Does this narrative have value for most of the students gathered here?" Have I covered the basic journalistic questions: Who? What? When? Where? Is the language choice specific and descriptive enough so that the audience can visualize the scenes? Have I been selective enough to omit unnecessary details? Are many transitions from scene to scene smooth?

**Model Speech
Personal
Experience**

Incident at Lacey Bridge

New Year's Day, 1978, is a day that I will never forget. It was a cold, quiet Sunday with the temperature at 1:00 p.m. about 30 degrees. My family and I had driven to a place called Lacey Bridge in our home town of Narragansett, Rhode Island. The bridge ran over a river whose water temperature was later estimated at 32 degrees.

We had come to Lacey Bridge to watch a group of winter swimming fanatics called the "Ice Cubes" begin the New Year by plunging off the bridge into the bitter waters below. I learned later that the "Cubes" were trying to outdo the more experienced "Polar Bears" who welcomed each New Year by charging into the Atlantic surf from a local beach.

A large crowd had gathered at the bridge and many of them clambered down the banks of the river where they could look up at the jumpers. I remember people waving and laughing to each other, wishing each other a "Happy New Year".

A few minutes after one o'clock, a husky young man dressed in sweat shirt and pants jumped up onto the wall of the bridge to announce the Ice Cubes' arrival. He entertained the crowd, joking while he shadowboxed precariously on the ledge of the bridge. A friend passed up a bottle of whisky and a long drink made him dance all the more. Suddenly, he was joined by another figure who climbed somewhat tentatively onto the ledge. He wore a "Cubes" shirt, tattered pants, and a colored Hawaiian lei around his neck — probably a souvenir from a New Year's Eve party.

Without a word, he launched himself into space and landed with a splash in the dark waters below. As soon as he surfaced, the current caught him, pulling him northward under the bridge. He tried to swim to the bank but was pulled in the other direction. I saw him disappear under the bridge and I assumed he would let the current take him to the other side of the bridge where he would climb out.

As this was happening, the rest of the Cubes began cannonballing into the water. The crowd whooped with delight as the jumpers landed, surfaced, and were helped ashore by their friends. It was then that I glimpsed the first leaper trying in vain to get out from under the bridge. Other people saw him too and sensed he was in trouble. I vividly remember a lady standing next to me saying, "Aren't we going to do anything? Are we just going to stand here and let that man drown?" In the confusion, all but one of us did nothing.

One man in all that crowd saw his responsibility and acted. Mark Gillooly, a 22-year-old college student, became concerned when he noticed the Hawaiian lei worn by the first leaper come floating out from under Lacey Bridge. He ran down to the bank on the north side just as a man's body emerged, face down in the water.

Gillooly immediately dove into the frigid waters and, holding a limp wrist of the almost dead leaper, he pulled him to shore. The novice Ice Cube was rushed to the hospital suffering from exposure and asphyxiation. He survived though doctors estimated another minute or more in the water might have been fatal.

Afterward, it was clear that Mark Gillooly had saved the leaper's life with his heroic act. What wasn't as clear, and yet just as certain, was that the same act of courage saved many of us who had stood immobilized on the banks of the river from having to absolve ourselves forever after of the guilt of inaction.

Later, I, along with others, would ask myself some difficult questions. Should I have gone into the icy waters after the helpless swimmer? Should we, a few of us, have formed a human chain to save him? The answers were unclear. The problem about being in a crowd, it seemed, was that individual responsibility became blurred. Fortunately, for both the leaper and all the spectators, one young college student was courageous enough to risk his own life for a fellow man he didn't even know. Think about it for a moment ... What would you have done?

Thank You.

Follow your instructor's directions for using this outline.

Outline of Speech

*Name:*_____

Title of Speech: _____

Purpose of Speech: _____

Type of Audience: _____

Time of Speech: _____

I. INTRODUCTION

    A.

        1.

        2.

    B.

        1.

        2.

    C.

        1.

        2.

II. BODY OF SPEECH

    A.

        1.

        2.

    B.

        1.

        2.

C.

    1.

    2.

D.

    1.

    2.

III. CONCLUSION

A.

    1.

    2.

B.

    1.

    2.

C.

    1.

    2.

D.

    1.

    2.

**The
Persuasive
Speech**

The most difficult and most challenging speech you will have to deliver is the persuasive speech.

Unlike the informative speech, the persuasive speech is not only seeking to give information, but to influence the attitudes, beliefs, and sometimes the behavior of the audience. For example, when President Franklin Delano Roosevelt delivered his famous war address to a joint session of Congress on December 8, 1941, he not only wanted to change the opinions of many Americans who did not want to become involved in a war in the Pacific, but to increase our military production and commitment of manpower in the Pacific. Other situations may call only for additudinal change. Public relations people are constantly engaged in efforts to secure "goodwill" for their clients even though they may not be trying to bring about any specific behavioral change.

Earlier (Points 1 & 2 — Preparing a Speech) you learned to choose a topic that you are personally interested in and to complete an audience analysis that reveals the values and attitudes that members of the audience are likely to have. These two points are particularly important to the success of a persuasive speech. Choose a topic you feel strongly about and then develop your themes, appeals, and arguments with the needs of your audience in mind. Show them how your position will benefit them directly.

Gordon Allport's classification system of value types might be helpful to you as you try to analyze present and future audiences. Essentially, the system breaks people down into categories according to the values that are of primary importance to individuals. This system will help you focus on the potential types that could be in your audience and this will allow you to fine-tune your message for your audience. Allport's system follows:

1/ The Theoretical Man: This type of person is concerned primarily with the empirical, critical, rational, and logical. He is necessarily an intellectualist and frequently becomes a *scientist or a philosopher.* His chief aim in life is to order and systematize his knowledge.

2/ The Economic Man: This type of person is primarily interested in what is useful. His interest develops to embrace the practical affairs of the business world — the production, marketing, and consumption of goods, the elaboration of credit, and the accumulation of tangible *wealth.* The economic attitude frequently comes into conflict with other values. Great feats of engineering, scientific management, and "applied psychology" result from the demands which economic men make upon learning.

3/ The Esthetic Man: The esthetic man sees his highest value in form and harmony. Each single experience is judged from the standpoint of grace, symmetry, or fitness. He need not be a creative artist ... his is esthetic if he but finds his chief interest in the artistic episodes of life.

4/ The Social Man: This type of person could be called the "Social Welfare Man." This person's highest value is *love* of people, whether of one or many, whether conjugal, filial, friendly, or philanthropic. The social man prizes other persons as ends, and is therefore himself kind, sympathetic, and unselfish. He is likely to find the theoretical, economic and esthetic attitudes as cold and inhuman.

5/ The Political Man: The political man is interested primarily in *power.* ... Since competition and struggle play a large part in all life, many philosophers have seen power as the most universal and most fundamental of motives. There are, however, certain personalities in whom the desire for a *direct* expression of this motive is uppermost, who wish above all else for personal power, influence, and renown.

6/ The Religious Man: The highest value for the religious man may be called unity. He is mystical, and seeks to comprehend the cosmos as a whole, to relate himself to its embracing totality.[2]

If you can determine the primary value of a particular audience, or if you can focus on several which seem to be manifested within your audience, you can create a more compelling message.

Format:

You can be effective as a persuasive speaker if you follow the suggestions that follow:

■ Stimulate interest in your topic during the introduction and establish the social, historical, or political context in which the issue is to be discussed. You may reveal your point-of-view at the outset if you feel your audience is sympathetic to your position. If, however, you feel there are members of the audience who will disagree with your position, it may be better to withhold your conclusion until the end after you have presented your reasons. Either way, you still have to support your argument.

- Use an inductive line of reasoning to support your position. This means that you will offer individual pieces of evidence that, when taken as a whole, will lead the open-minded members of the audience to accept your more general conclusion.

- Present evidence that has both quantity and quality. Factual evidence in sufficient quantity that is taken from quality sources is difficult to resist. By quality sources, we mean reputable written sources or people or organizations who are considered experts on your subject. Offer your facts in a logical sequence and keep your most powerful points for last.

- When appropriate, blend in emotional appeals with factual evidence but avoid being melodramatic or unethical.

- Explain how things will be better if your position is accepted, or describe the negative scenario that accompanies the opposite position.

- Conclude by trying to obtain the desired result. If it is attitudinal change you are after, ask for it. If it is action you want, tell the audience what to do and how to do it. Very often it will be both attitudinal and behavioral change that is your goal. When that occurs total persuasion has taken place. You have done your job well.

**Model Speech
Persuasive**

Take Your College in Stride
William G. Carleton

Professor William G. Carleton delivered this address at a meeting of first year students, mostly veterans, at the University of Florida, Gainesville, Florida, on November 25, 1946.

This speech is in almost every sense a model for school and college speechmakers. It is brief, original in concept and expression, personal and direct in audience appeal, well organized, filled with suggestions of humor and appreciation of campus associations, including faculty, students and library. It includes motivative elements that supplement the logical propositions stated or implied.

College offers you five great opportunities — professors, contact with fellow students who themselves are the

products of winnowing process, laboratories, a library
filled with books, and leisure time. And the greatest of
these is leisure time.

It is not strange that the greatest good provided by a
university is something intangible — something that cannot be seen, something that cannot be written down in
catalogues or reduced to clock hours, credits, degrees?
But the leisure time offered you during your university
days is the priceless boon. Never again in your life will you
have so much time — time to browse, to think, to dream,
to discuss, to argue, to question, to create, to construct.
Even if you should become a college professor you will
never again have so much precious leisure. Beware of
those educators who want to put you in a straightjacket
and make you account for every minute of your waking
hours. Those educators do not want a university; they
want an army.

What any professor can give you in any subject is limited — limited by the inability of any man, however great
his sense of the vicarious, to impart but a small fraction of
his knowledge and experience; limited by the necessarily
formal nature of the student-teacher relationship; limited
by the professor's own talents and background; limited by
cultural and traditional restraints. Even the greatest of
teachers are limited, limited by the very clarity of the point
of view which brings them to prominence and makes them
"great."

Your professor, to be sure, will be able to suggest, to
encourage, to help tie up loose ends, to put things together, to point out connections where none seemed to
exist before. If he is the sort of person who can do this in
an interesting and exciting way, so much the better. If he
has developed enough maturity in his own subject to have
come to a definite point of view and to have made some
original contributions, then you are blessed. And if he can
impart his ideas without pomposity and with humor and
sparkle, then you are twice blessed.

However, even the most gifted professors can give you
little real insight, understanding, ripeness of judgment, or
wisdom. These are the results of living, countless con-
tacts with men and events, wide experience, travel, observation, the reading of great books, the doing of great
deeds, and thinking and acting in real life situations.

The library, even in this scientific age, is the student's

chief source of knowledge. A university library is a truly wonderful place. There you can find almost all the ideas that men in all times and places have thought — the ugly and the beautiful, the foolish and the wise, the grotesque and the sensible, the curious and the useful. There you can relive the life experience of the race — the story, still unfinished, of man's slow groping for civilization.

As sources of ideas, professors simply cannot compete with books. Books can be found to fit almost every need, temper, or interest. Books can be read when you are in the mood; they do not have to be taken in periodic doses. Books are both more personal and more impersonal than professors. Books have an inner confidence which individuals seldom show: they rarely have to be on the defensive. Books can afford to be bold and courageous and exploratory; they do not have to be so careful of boards of trustees, colleagues, and community opinion. Books are infinitely diverse; they run the gamut of human activity. Books can be found to express every point of view; if you want a different point of view you can read a different book. (Incidentally, this is the closest approximation to objectivity you are likely ever to get in humanistic and social studies.) Even your professor is at his best when he writes books and articles; the teaching performance rarely equals the written effort.

Students who come to the university merely to learn a trade will not understand what I have had to say. Neither will those who come merely to earn high grades or deliberately to make Phi Beta Kappa. But the others — those who have come to learn of life in this puzzling and complicated world of ours — will, I think, understand.

Reprinted by permission of "Vital Speeches of the Day."

Follow your instructor's directions for using this outline.

Outline of Speech

*Name:*_____

Title of Speech: _____

Purpose of Speech: _____

Type of Audience: _____

Time of Speech: _____

I. INTRODUCTION

    A.

        1.

        2.

    B.

        1.

        2.

    C.

        1.

        2.

II. BODY OF SPEECH

    A.

        1.

        2.

    B.

        1.

        2.

  C.

    1.

    2.

  D.

    1.

    2.

III. CONCLUSION

  A.

    1.

    2.

  B.

    1.

    2.

  C.

    1.

    2.

  D.

    1.

    2.

7

SPEECHES FOR SPECIAL OCCASIONS

We live in a society in which ceremony and ritual have become a daily part of our behavioral patterns. More often than not, these occasions require individuals to deliver speeches appropriate to the ceremony or ritual. These special occasion speeches differ from each other. However, they share something in common in that each situation has certain *expectations* that the speaker must meet. If you learn what is expected, establish a formulaic approach to fulfill the expectations, and apply the principles of public speaking you have already acquired, you will be prepared for any occasion. This last point needs to be stressed because, often, you will not be given much time to prepare your remarks.

Certain general principles apply to all special occasion speeches. You need to be consistent with the appropriate tone or mood the situation calls for; you should be brief (1-3 minutes) without rushing, and you should remember that your role is subordinate to the ceremony's primary purpose, whatever it may be.

Introductions

When you are called on to introduce another speaker, the expectations for such a speech are quite clear. You are expected to provide information about the speaker and his topic and, in so doing, establish a friendly and warm atmosphere in which the speaker and audience can relate to each other. To do this, follow this formula. Ideally, you will use only the briefest of notes.

- Welcome audience and refer to the purpose of the occasion.

- Provide the name and background of the speaker. Here, it helps to have done your homework researching the speaker's position, education, experience, and accomplishments. Be selective and include only significant data. (If you have advance notice and no other way of obtaining information, you may ask the speaker to send you a short, biographical sketch.) Do not overdo the build-up.

- Explain why the subject of the talk is meaningful to the audience and what they stand to gain from listening.

- Conclude by repeating the name of the speaker and his topic. Be certain you are able to pronounce the speaker's name correctly.

**Model
Introduction
Speech**

Good morning, ladies and gentlemen of the faculty. Welcome back to our annual faculty orientation day at Hastings College. I hope you are all tanned and rested, eager to go back to work teaching our students who will be returning to campus this Wednesday.

To start the new academic year off on the right track, we have invited Doctor Martha Munroe to speak to you this morning. Doctor Munroe comes to us with a distinguished academic and professional background. She received a Bachelor's degree in Communications from Northwestern University and a Ph.D. from Stanford University. For the past eight years, she has been a communications consultant to businesses and government agencies. She has also found time to author four books, one of which, *Take Time to Talk,* is presently on the top ten best-selling, non-fiction books.

Doctor Munroe's topic, "Communication Channels in Classrooms," could not be more suitable. It is our hope that Doctor Munroe's remarks will act as a catalyst so that we can greet our students on Wednesday with fresh and enthusiastic approaches.

Ladies and gentlemen, I present to you Doctor Martha Munroe speaking on "Communication Channels in Classrooms".

Follow your instructor's directions for using this outline.

Outline of Speech

*Name:*_____

Title of Speech: _____

Purpose of Speech: _____

Type of Audience: _____

Time of Speech: _____

I. INTRODUCTION

    A.

        1.

        2.

    B.

        1.

        2.

    C.

        1.

        2.

II. BODY OF SPEECH

    A.

        1.

        2.

    B.

        1.

        2.

    C.

      1.

      2.

    D.

      1.

      2.

III. CONCLUSION

    A.

      1.

      2.

    B.

      1.

      2.

    C.

      1.

      2.

    D.

      1.

      2.

**Speeches of
Presentation**

From our earliest years, we have participated in ceremonies where achievements are recognized by the presentation of awards. The award may vary from Little League trophies to scholarships for academic excellence, but the ritual remains the same. Similar ceremonies are held by corporations. Awards are presented to outstanding salespeople, managers, and those who make special contributions to their community. Many companies present gifts to retiring employees in gratitude for years of loyal service. Because these situations occur so frequently in our culture, the expectations for the speech of presentation have become commonly accepted.

Formula:

- Explain the background, significance, and criteria for the award.

- Point out what the recipient(s) has done to merit the award.

- Ask the recipient to come up to physically accept the award.

- Present the award with your left hand so that your right hand is free for a congratulatory handshake.

**Model Speech
of Presentation**

The Garnett Award is given each year to a student who best balances academic achievement with meaningful extracurricular involvement. The award consists of a $500 check and a plaque commemorating the achievement. This is the twentieth year that the Garnett Award has been given since it was begun by a distinguished alumnus, Mr. Orville Garnett, founder and president of Garnett Industries.

This year's recipient is Harold Brown, who comes to us from New Orleans, Louisiana. As a junior majoring in marketing, Harold has maintained a 3.8 cumulative average since his freshman year. Also he has lettered in varsity basketball and tennis, served on the yearbook staff as a copy editor, been president of the Marketing Club, and treasurer of the local DECA chapter. If that isn't enough, Harold is also a volunteer in the campus Outreach program which sponsors visits and work sessions to the Whitestone Center. Here, Harold and other volunteers work with retarded children.

Would Harold Brown please come forward to receive the Garnett Award which he so clearly deserves.

Follow your instructor's directions for using this outline.

Outline of Speech

*Name:*_____

Title of Speech: _____

Purpose of Speech: _____

Type of Audience: _____

Time of Speech: _____

I. INTRODUCTION

   A.

      1.

      2.

   B.

      1.

      2.

   C.

      1.

      2.

II. BODY OF SPEECH

   A.

      1.

      2.

   B.

      1.

      2.

C.

    1.

    2.

D.

    1.

    2.

III. CONCLUSION

A.

    1.

    2.

B.

    1.

    2.

C.

    1.

    2.

D.

    1.

    2.

Speech of Acceptance

If you are fortunate enough to receive an award, you had better be prepared to make an acceptance speech because, more often than not, you will be asked to do just that. There is no graceful way to refuse and to do so would certainly spoil the moment. It is better to do what is expected of you in a sincere and appreciative way.

Formula:

- Thank both those who are giving you an award and those responsible for creating the award.

- Express your appreciation to the people who were instrumental in helping you win the award.

- Close by repeating your thanks. This speech is usually quite brief.

Model Speech of Acceptance

I wish to thank the faculty members who selected me to be the recipient of the Garnett Award. Also I am grateful to Mr. Garnett and his company for their generosity.

Winning the award is, of course, a thrill. I am aware that I owe a debt of gratitude to the teachers, coaches, and to my fellow students whom I have enjoyed learning from and being with during the past three years.

Again, thank you very much.

Follow your instructor's directions for using this outline.

Outline of Speech

Name: _____

Title of Speech: _____

Purpose of Speech: _____

Type of Audience: _____

Time of Speech: _____

I. INTRODUCTION

    A.

        1.

        2.

    B.

        1.

        2.

    C.

        1.

        2.

II. BODY OF SPEECH

    A.

        1.

        2.

    B.

        1.

        2.

C.

1.

2.

D.

1.

2.

III. CONCLUSION

A.

1.

2.

B.

1.

2.

C.

1.

2.

D.

1.

2.

Announcements

Many times the announcement of an important event, company policy, or occurrence is relegated to an inexperienced speaker or placed at the end of a program when people are not likely to listen. It is unfortunate that announcements are treated as afterthoughts. If you have an important announcement to make, have it prepared, make copies of it to be distributed immediately afterward or that same day through inter-office mail, and do not make the announcement at the end of a program or meeting. You should make all important announcements at the beginning.

Keep the announcement brief and get to the point(s) quickly. The "journalistic" questions of the public relations practitioner should be your guiding principles when you deliver the message. They are: *WHO? WHAT? WHEN? WHERE? WHY?* and sometimes *HOW?* Your audience should not be left questioning what is happening or what they should be doing with your information.

Formula:

- Get the attention of the audience and quickly preview the purpose of the announcement.

- Make the announcement providing all necessary facts (dates, times, places, amounts, etc.).

- If possible, ask for and respond to any questions from the audience.

- Repeat details and close on a motivational note.

Model Speech of Announcement

Every year, at this time, all the employees of the Brown Company have an opportunity to assist our fellow man by contributing to the United Way. For the past three years, we have had the highest percentage of people who contribute through payroll deductions of any firm in the city. We would like to continue this record.

Here is all you have to do. Return the contribution card that will be in the mail this week to Pat Bourne in the Payroll Office by November 1st. Indicate the amount you want deducted. It is that simple. Remember, besides, helping others in the community, you will be entered in the annual Bermuda drawing which provides an all-expenses paid week-for-two on Bermuda.

Are there any questions?

Fine, get the United Way card back to Pat Bourne in Payroll by November 1st. Your donation is tax-deductible and you are helping a worthwhile cause.

Thank You.

Follow your instructor's directions for using this outline.

Outline of Speech

*Name:*_____

Title of Speech: _____

Purpose of Speech: _____

Type of Audience: _____

Time of Speech: _____

I. INTRODUCTION

  A.

   1.

   2.

  B.

   1.

   2.

  C.

   1.

   2.

II. BODY OF SPEECH

  A.

   1.

   2.

  B.

   1.

   2.

    C.

       1.

       2.

    D.

       1.

       2.

III. CONCLUSION

    A.

       1.

       2.

    B.

       1.

       2.

    C.

       1.

       2.

    D.

       1.

       2.

THREE MODEL SPEECHES FOR STUDENTS PLANNING BUSINESS CAREERS

What They Should Have Told Me When I Was a Senior
Learn to Spell and Write Please
Rebecca C. Jann, Assistant Professor of Biology, Queens College

Delivered as an address for Senior Recognition Day, Charlotte, North Carolina, September 13, 1983.

Greetings to you, seniors, who invited me to address you today and who soon will be able to decide whether that was a mistake. Greetings to you, colleagues, and to you, freshmen, and most special greetings to anyone who came even though you were not required to.

When I was facing my senior year, I needed some good answers fast, and nobody would give me any. I was just beginning to be a little bit receptive to some good answers ... because I had conscientiously avoided following any advice at all for a couple of decades and now I was facing some of the consequences.

For example, since I had changed my major six times, the only way I could graduate with a major in my new and true calling was to schedule six labs per week during my last year. Having six labs is pretty bad, but what was worse was that several of the required courses were not about anything I really needed to know.

I realized that even if I managed to graduate, I was going to be facing the hard, cruel world knowing practically nothing about the really important parts of science — like volcanos and dinosaurs and, of course, sex.

I went to the library and checked out a lot of books on volcanos and dinosaurs and, of course, sex. I couldn't read the books during lab and get them all smeared with substances you would rather not hear about, and I couldn't read them in the evening because I had some critical extracurricular activities to maintain (co-ed school). We weren't allowed to cut lectures; so I just sat toward the back in most of my irrelevant classes and read the books about volcanos and dinosaurs and ... whatever.

Naturally, then I had some problems about QPAs and letters of recommendation and so forth.

When I was a senior I was about ready to admit my mistakes and be more receptive to advice for the future, like how to cope with the real world after graduation and whether I should go to graduate school, and if so, where? Or maybe should I get a job, and, if so, what and how? Or should I just get married and if so, to whom?

I wanted those answers fast. That's when I got the bad news: there were no answers after graduation. But that was a long time ago, and now ... we still don't have any answers.

I could end with that message, but I won't. I'm tempted to. Maybe there are no absolute truths to help you make decisions about life during your senior year and after graduation, but I have compiled two lists of nearly indisputable certainties.

My first list comes from my professional knowledge as a biologist. These are ten facts which I think everybody could find useful in making decisions about the future. These are facts important especially for those of you who are going to escape without taking my courses. These are facts which are 99.9 percent certain.

1. The human brain will function properly only within a healthy human body because the brain depends on a critical balance of natural psychoactive drugs which the body makes. Without the proper chemical balance, the brain tries to make you do the wrong things.

2. The human body is designed for regular activity. Without regular exercise, its natural drug balance gets messed up and your brain tries to make you do the wrong things.

3. There is no way to lose weight quickly and safely.

4. You can't keep frogs alive in captivity for more than two weeks.

5. Smoking is bad for you. Actually it doesn't matter what you are smoking or even sniffing, it is bad for you.

6. Carbohydrates are good for you.

7. To keep your houseplants healthy, try to give them a home which closely imitates their natural habitat. Unfortunately, this means you have to find out where they came from.

8. We do have a real problem with the environment — accumulations of toxic pesticides and industrial wastes in our country and overpopulation in many parts of the world and dwindling energy sources everywhere. If we don't make the right decisions about the environment now, you won't have much of a future to worry about. The very least you can do about it is to learn as much as you can about these problems and then to vote responsibly and to write your legislators.

9. Women really are different from men, not just in the obvious anatomical features but also in the way our brains work. For many years, I didn't want to believe this fact, but now I see that the fact that our brains work differently is a compelling reason to insist that we gain a larger role in running the world.

10. This fact is known to students in my physiology class as Jann's second law: You are what you think you are. I already told you that your body controls the drug balance of your brain. Equally important is knowing that your brain controls the hormones and nerves of your body. If that sounds like catch 22, it is. The worse you feel, the worse you feel, and vice versa. On the other side of the coin, this means that the human brain is capable of helping you overcome disease and anatomical deficiencies. Miracle cures do exist, but only if you believe in them, and you can be one of the world's most beautiful women or one of the world's most successful women or one of the world's greatest minds only if you believe in yourself.

My second list of ten near-absolute certainties comes from personal experience. Actually, I am only 97.5 percent sure of some of these certainties, and those of you who have more personal experience than I are not required to listen.

1. You don't have to learn everything from first-hand experience. Many 99 percent certainties can come from the experience of others as revealed to you through conversations with friends and through great literature, visual art, and music and maybe even soaps. If I didn't believe

this certainty, that you don't have to learn everything from first-hand experience, I wouldn't be making this speech.

2. The only valid reason to get married is for love.

3. The way you can tell if it's really love is to try to live without being with him. If you survive, then you know it wasn't really true love.

4. The only valid way to choose a career is for love.

5. The way you can tell you have a career is if you can hardly wait to get to work. If you dread going to work most days, then you don't have a career; you have a job ... and you might as well look for another job which is easier or which pays better. For many very happy and successful people, jobs are just ways to finance their true callings. Their real careers are what they do in their spare time.

6. If you dread going to class but you're doing it so you can have a career or even a job, you'd better be prepared for a big disappointment. There were people who liked the classes I dreaded, the classes where I sat in the back and read books. The people who liked the classes I dreaded ended up in careers very different from mine. The classes and subjects and activities and people you like are very good predictors of the type of career you will love. If you have never liked any of your classes, there's good news. There are very few jobs available in those fields anyway. According to several reliable sources, the only college graduates who are virtually guaranteed of a career for the rest of this century are those who are majoring in nursing. For the rest of you, it's too late to change your major. The other top ten employment opportunities for the rest of this century are in fields like retail sales and driving trucks and fast foods. So your best bet is to find out what you like and make a career of it, even if your job is just your way to finance your true calling.

7. The most important job skill in any career suitable for a college graduate is good writing. If you really want to go for it, use your senior year wisely. Beg your instructors to assign term papers and urge them to write critical comments in the margins.

8. Honesty is the best policy.

9. (I counted wrong, because I like math.)

10. Careers are less important than personal relationships. However, the people I know who have great personal relationships are the ones who have real careers,

either in their jobs or in their spare time.

In summary, here is my advice for you to use during your senior year: Eat right, get lots of exercise, don't inhale anything except the cleanest air you can find, and don't make any decisions until you are sure your brain's drug balance is stable.

Next semester, take as many courses as Dean Thompson will allow. Find out what you like, and then spend your time learning so much about it that your brain convinces you and the rest of the world that you are A-one, top-notch, and totally awesome.

Learn to spell and write. Please.

If you are married or insist on getting married, remember that for centuries men have neglected their personal relationships and their health and their brains' natural drug balances to pursue their careers. Now that you have the opportunity to make the same mistakes, don't.

For those of you who are curious about what happened during and after my senior year, I did finally graduate. I turned down a graduate fellowship and got married and had 2.2 children. I read all my husband's textbooks for the courses I didn't get to take. I had brief careers as a carpenter and as a semi-pro musician and a fairly long career as a nearly full-time volunteer. Then I got another graduate fellowship and became a retread. I had limited careers in teaching various sciences to people of various levels of ability and interest; and I had brief careers in biological research and in environmental consulting. I'm still happily married to a very fine man who finances my many careers and supports me in many other ways. Now here I am being what I think I am.

Three Career Traps for Women
Caution: Your Career May Be Hazardous to Your Health

Bonita L. Perry, Communicator Psychologist, Sun Company
Delivered to the American Women in Radio and Television, Philadelphia, Pennsylvania, October 20, 1981

When JFK was asked why he wanted to become president, he replied, "Because that's where the power is." Well, that's true of course, but that's not the only place the power is. In fact presidents of recent vintage would readily acknowledge that it's the President and Congress working together that is really powerful. And they'd probably just as readily admit that one other significant power base in this country is the media.

That puts you in a pretty powerful position. Indirectly or directly, you determine what the world will talk about, read about, worry about and delight in.

What I'd like to consider today is how much of our power — yours and mine — do we use to determine the course of our own personal and professional lives.

My comments today are aimed at women who are and have been engaged in careers. Women who are pursuing those careers full steam ahead: who are making sacrifices for those careers and who are paying the price of achieving power, climbing the ladder and gaining influence in the business and corporate world.

I will speak from two vantage points: my educational background in psychology and my professional experience as a Management Consultant with Booz, Allen & Hamilton, and as a fairly high-level Manager at the 18th largest U.S. corporation, Sun Company.

There are three career traps women seem to get caught up in. Hopefully, by being more aware of them, you can minimize the risks of these adverse conditions so you can maximize the rewards of your careers. The three traps I will discuss today I have labeled: The Perfectionism Trap, The Burn-Out Blues, and Seduction by Security. Along the way, I will give you a little quiz that I think you will find fun and helpful. Hopefully, I will spark some questions and comments for a discussion afterward.

First, there is *The Perfectionism Trap.* Actually, men as well as women get ensnared by it, but women seem to be particularly vulnerable. This reflects, I think, our conviction that the pressure is still on us to prove ourselves and our capabilities in the business world.

"What is perfectionism?" It is not the healthy pursuit of excellence by men and women who take genuine pleasure in striving to meet high standards. This is necessary for quality life, marked by true accomplishments. Perfectionism is setting standards which are unnaturally high beyond reach or reason. It is straining compulsively and unremittingly toward impossible goals. It is measuring self-worth entirely in terms of productivity and accomplishment. It is a compulsive effort to excel in all things.

To some extent, perfectionism is a cultural phenomenon. We are afraid of being mediocre or average. No one wants to be average — of average ability, of average intelligence, of average potential or of average looks. Our language patterns reinforce these beliefs. We talk about "the perfect evening" or "the perfect meal" or "the perfect marriage." A camera ad I saw recently said "experience the sense of perfection." Perfectionism thinking is all about us.

However, when we adopt this approach toward our work, it creates risks we don't need and jeopardizes the extent to which our careers can be rewarding. Here are three ways that I have observed women express their quest to be perfect at work.

Number one is Disclosure Phobia. There is a fear of showing our real selves. A fear that if our boss really knew us, the gig would be up. This fear is based in a worry about what others think of us. We want them to think that we are more than we are, that we are more perfect than we feel. We have a fear of appearing foolish or inadequate resulting in a reluctance to participate in meetings or to share our ideas openly. In addition, we resist sharing our inner thoughts or feelings. We think our human foibles will not be accepted by others and we are excessively sensitive to real or imagined disapproval by others.

The result for women who fear disclosing information about themselves is that they usually appear cold and aloof, non-participating and distant, insensitive and uncaring. In fact, these assumptions others make about women who disclose very little are often worse than if they had spoken out and disclosed more about themselves and their ideas. This kind of behavior deprives women of intimate communication. The warmth and unconditional acceptance they crave can never be earned through accomplishment. It can only come about through our own openness and the quality of our interpersonal relationships.

The second way I have observed women to behave in a perfectionistic mode is to set excessively high standards for others in addition to themselves.

They expect their subordinates and peers to perform at the same high levels as they do. They expect them to have the same high standards that they do. They fail to recognize that excelling and achieving at work is not as important to some employees as it may be to them.

Therefore, when others don't live up to their excessively high standards, they are inevitably disappointed and react with annoyance. The subordinate usually reacts back to this judgmental attitude with resentment. The perfectionist then becomes even more demanding and both parties end up exasperated.

My third observation is that perfectionists perceive themselves as having a very narrow margin of safety. They fear, "one error, one mistake, no matter how small and I am finished." I see some women at work who play it safe all the time. They fear making even a small mistake or violating a company rule and this keeps them from trying new things, taking some risks and ultimately gaining new skills and competencies and the confidence that goes with them.

It is this perception of having a very narrow margin of safety that can keep us from taking the risks we need to for personal and career growth.

These are but three of the many behavior patterns we can get into when we seek to be perfect. All of this adds up to a set of very unpleasant circumstances for perfection-minded working women. We take on more work than we can effectively handle. We work under unrealistic deadlines. We alienate co-workers and subordinates. We don't build the interpersonal relationships that can help us deal with the stress and pressures of our jobs, and we don't let ourselves make mistakes. And that's just on the job. Off the job, we often have our sights set on being the best cook, the best tennis player, and the most sparkling conversationalist.

What can you do to head off these tendencies or reduce them if you felt an uncomfortable tinge of awareness as I spoke?

Dare to be average. Dwell on the pleasures of mediocrity. Accept the fact that there is no way any one of us can be superior in everything that we do. We can excel in some activities but we don't need to in everything we do.

On this point, Laurence Peter, of the Peter Principle fame, said, "Most hierarchies were established by men who now monopolize the upper levels, thus depriving women of their rightful share of opportunities to achieve incompetence."

My point is this: we don't have to excel in every part of our jobs or our personal lives. We can make mistakes, we can have foibles, we can be human. And in the end we will succeed because of it.

The second trap I see career women susceptible to is what I call *The Burn-Out Blues.*

Again, it isn't uniquely a feminine problem. But women seem to be particularly vulnerable to it as we broaden our position in the workforce today.

What is burn-out? In its simplest terms, psychologists say, it is a condition produced by working too hard, too long in a high pressure environment.

From another perspective, burn-out has been defined as the high cost of high achievement. In a book with that title, Dr. Herbert J. Freudenberger argues that society itself is the breeder of burn-out. It results from an incompatibility in the relationships of the individual to society. Society continues to dangle impossible dreams before us. But at the very same time, it is eroding the traditions and weakening the support systems and relationships that are essential in achieving goals.

There are several types of women that I see as potential burn-out candidates:

The Super Woman — She tries to fulfill all roles to all people: wife, mother, friend, lover, employee, boss, subordinate — the woman who keeps adding roles as if more is somehow better.

The Listening Ear Woman — The one who listens to everyone else's problems, who always has time for others, who is always giving but seldom getting anything back.

The Workaholic — Those who put their work before all else in their lives, who become unidimensional, who lack multiple sources of gratification in their lives.

The Challengeaholic — Who is constantly looking for new mountains to climb, who cannot enjoy the plateaus before seeking new heights.

The Misplaced Person — Who simply doesn't fit the job anymore.

Whatever the type of candidate, the results are the same: overcommitment, no time for self, frustration, resentment, fatigue, boredom and finally a sense of enuii — nothing seems to matter anymore. Recognizing the early symptoms of burn-out can help to avoid serious problems later. Now it's time for the quiz. I will read 15 questions. Please consider each of them in terms of how much change has occurred in you and your feelings on this matter over the past six months. Then jot down a number from a 1 to 5 scale for each question, with 1 representing no change or little change and 5 standing for a great deal of change.

Here are the 15 questions contained in a test framed by Dr. Freudenberger.

1. Do you tire more easily and feel fatigued a lot, rather than feeling energetic?

2. Are people annoying you by saying you don't look so good lately?

3. Are you working more and more and accomplishing less and less?

4. Are you becoming more cynical and disenchanted with things around you?

5. Do you often feel a sadness you can't explain?

6. Are you more forgetful — about appointments, deadlines and your personal possessions?

7. Are you more irritable, short-tempered and disappointed in the people around you?

8. Are you seeing close friends and family less frequently?

9. Are you too busy for even routine things such as making telephone calls and sending out Christmas cards?

10. Are you suffering from physical complaints — aches, pains, headaches or a lingering cold?

11. Do you feel disoriented when the day's activities come to a halt?

12. Are joy and happiness elusive?

13. Are you unable to laugh at a joke about yourself.

14. Does sex seem like it's more trouble than it's worth?

15. Do you have very little to say to people?

Now, total the numbers you jotted down and I will give you the scoring to position yourself on the *Burn-Out Scale.*

If your total is from 0 to 25 points, you are doing fine ... 26 to 35 points means there are some things you should be watching ... 36 to 50 points identifies you as a candidate for burn-out ... 51 to 65 points means you are to some degree now burning-out … and a score over 65 is in the nature of red alert, suggesting that you are behaving in ways that are threatening to your physical and mental well-being.

What can you do about it? Some suggestions:

First, limit — really limit — the amount of time you work. And set aside some special time for activities that you find relaxing.

Second, take vacations. Mini-vacations and weekend get-aways count too. Don't get involved in the "not having time to do it" trap.

Third, find support — other women or men with whom you can communicate or commiserate and with whom you can problem-solve.

Fourth, promote the team approach to work. Ask for help when you need it, delegate work to others and trust your associates and subordinates.

Fifth, stop searching for the Big Reward that will some-how solve all of your problems and make everything worthwhile. Satisfaction really comes from the blending of many small rewards — a pat on the back from the boss, a complimentary handshake from a friend, a word of thanks from a husband — those are part and parcel of our daily lives.

Avoiding burn-out is largely a matter of perspective. And I like this perspective contributed by American humorist Kim Hubbard: "Do not take life too seriously; you will never get out of it alive."

I've labeled my third trap: *Seduction by Security.*

In comparison with the other two, it might be considered a downside risk since it is concerned with attempting not too much but too little.

The problem arises because some degree of security is attractive to all of us. After working for a time in one job in one organization we build up a considerable degree of security in such things as pension benefits, high salary levels and expectations, seniority and comfortable in-dividual and organizational relationships. And that secu-rity is fine as long as it doesn't blind us to the change that is continuously taking place in us and around us.

Let's look at some of those changes.

Individually, we choose a career field early in life. Then, as the years pass, our interests and our values and our needs change. At some point, we may no longer have a vocational "fit." And we may suddenly realize at age 30 or 40 that we are working at a job selected for us by some 18-year-old. Our interests and capabilities simply don't fit with the requirements and opportunities of the job anymore.

Our roles and relationships within our organizations change, too. A common change is the move from a position requiring technical and professional expertise to one involving the managing of people and organizational units. When that move occurs, the world changes sharply for the new manager.

My suggestion to you is that change demands that we regularly and realistically appraise the fit between ourselves, our jobs and our organizations. Just like a pair of shoes that doesn't fit properly, a job that doesn't fit us any more is painful. We shouldn't stay just because it is a known entity. Sometimes we prefer the security of the known, no matter how unpleasant and painful it may be, to the insecurity of the unknown, the new opportunity.

As Will Rogers once said, "Even if you're on the right track, you'll get run over if you just sit there."

I suggest we carefully monitor what's happening in our organizations and in our jobs and how we feel about it. And when the fit is no longer comfortable, we must face the facts and initiate a change. This in no way means that we have failed — or that our organizations have failed us. It simply means that a normal process of change is taking place and that we are aware of it and we are adjusting to it.

Thomas Carlyle summed up the importance of a vocational fit in a way that is meaningful to me. He said and I have changed the pronouns, "Blessed is she who has found her work: for she needs no other blessing."

I would like to add an observation about risks and risking.

It is said today that people increasingly tend to play it safe in all areas of their lives. And that is particularly true of women. If this is true, it may result from the fact that we are still uncomfortably close to some of the barriers we had to climb over in getting to where we now are in the business and communications worlds — and that we do not wish to place at risk the gains that we have already won.

In a broader sense, however, risk cannot really be

avoided. Building a meaningful, successful career demands that we pursue excellence and strive to achieve at high levels. In doing so we face the risk of going too far and becoming perfectionists ... or of trying to do too much and burning out midway through our careers ... or of emphasizing too heavily the retention of what we've got as opposed to moving to something that fits us better.

In closing, I suggest that we weave into our career perspectives these words from the courageous Helen Keller. She said:

"Security is mostly a superstition. It does not exist in nature, nor do the children of men as a whole experience it. Avoiding danger is no safer in the long run than outright exposure. Life is either a daring adventure or nothing."

I suggest that choosing between these two outcomes — a "daring adventure" or "nothing" — is not a difficult choice.

Model Speech

Management by Inspiration
A Few Simple Reminders

George F. Burns, President of Consumer Products Division,
SCM Corporation
Delivered at the Durkee Famous Foods Sales Conference,
Lincolnshire, Illinois, August 9, 1982

GOOD MORNING. I'm very happy to be here with you today. First, my congratulations. Your efforts made it a great year for *Durkee Famous Foods.* As you know, this year was the best in our history. I'm pleased and proud of all of you. My sincere congratulations and deepest appreciation to Bill Miller, John Lowrie, Tom Stuckart, and each of you.

Now, I'll say no more about the past year or even our plans for the future. Others will provide particulars on them and on making next year even more successful!

Today I'd like to talk from a more personal perspective, on a topic that's vital to good business management, and to SCM.

As you may know I'll be retiring in December after 37 years with the company. Naturally at this stage of a career, you look back and try, if possible, to put it in perspective. And reflecting my experiences, I have some good sense of what makes people work and how they might be inspired to excel. We all have within us the power to succeed, the goal is to release it; in ourselves and in others.

The word inspiration comes from the Latin and means, to give life, to breath into, to put spirit into as God does to Adam in Genesis. Inspiration is a state of mind that's linked to productivity, in the sense that inspired artists are likely to produce better works of art. Imagine how Michelangelo felt as he contemplated painting the Sistine Chapel. There is a vital relationship between inspiration and production. In business, inspiration is often called motivation — a more recent term for the force that moves people to perform well, even under difficult conditions.

Just what is it that inspires a person to create or perform with excellence? There are external things like money, status, and power. For some, they are the spur to fame and fortune. But true inspiration is water from a deeper well. It comes from believing in yourself. It's a sense of self-worth and of pride that you get from working hard and accomplishing things.

Remember the scene in the film *Chariots of Fire* where the runner asks himself "Where does the power come from to run the race to the end?" His answer: "The power comes from within." Of course, inspiration can also come from others. We are often inspired by heros whether artists, athletes, or astronauts. These individuals can serve as role models and, on occasion, as teachers.

A man named Saul Yaffa hired me as a Smith-Corona salesman back in 1945. Saul was soft spoken and always a gentle man. At the outset he said to me: "George you can read all the books, and study your product till midnight. I can teach you the business and teach you how to work. But there's one thing I can't do — and that's make you want to work."

And Yaffa was a good teacher in the days before sophisticated sales training techniques were developed. Here's one of his favorite techniques. Everyday, when you're finished, perhaps tired, and ready to quit, make one more call. Keep a record of these "extra" calls. And if the call is bad, make another one and keep going till you get a prospect. This way you not only go home on a high note, but you've structured your day with an upward momentum instead of just winding down. The ultimate call becomes something you psyche yourself up for. You leave feeling good about yourself and your work, ready to run again the next day.

This particular approach may or may not work for every individual. What makes a great salesman is something more natural: self-inspiration. It's a personal desire, a primary impulse to get going without anybody telling you. If you're self-inspired, you're halfway there. Anybody can be taught tactics but the drive to win comes from within.

When I say self-inspiration is natural, I don't mean you're born with it. It's part of your nature because you put it there. How do you inspire yourself? Each person does it differently, but all of us have something in our make-up that triggers action. To find it, you must know yourself and be honest about your life's ambitions. Socrates challenged his students to know themselves and Plato suggested that an unexamined life wasn't worth living.

Inspiration, through self-awareness, is essential for success in any demanding endeavor whether it's selling or skiing. Selling is a dynamic, challenging job. Unfortunately, it's among the less understood and unappreciated professions. The old image of the fast-talking, cigar smoking huckster is due for an overhaul. You can find dishonest individuals in any line of work including selling. I believe the salesman has become an important national figure. America could not have become the rich and productive nation it is without people selling its products. No matter what you produce, we all know nothing happens until a sale is made. That is our moment of truth.

You have to be smart to sell well. Selling involves technical knowledge and interpersonal skills. Even in an age of automation, the sales force remains the backbone of a business organization. If your front line troops fail to move products, the battle's over, the company's dead.

Now it appears, that I'm preaching to the converted, but at times there's an exhilaration in rediscovering the truth behind clichés we hear. There's a lot of talk about the emerging era of leisure and new industries have sprung up offering recreational goods and services. Some say hard work, as we know it, will become passé in a computerized society. Describing a "postindustrial" society where most people will work at home through computers, Alvin Toffler says: "We are moving toward a future economy in which very large numbers will never hold full-time paid jobs." He claims that the distinction between work and leisure will disappear.

That might be true by the year 2082, but today leisure exists in the context of work, and without this framework, leisure can become decadence. The fact remains that work gives meaning to life. It provides a sense of mastery and achievement thus, enhanced self-worth. Recreation complements vocation. Work hard, play hard. But work before play. Why? Well here's how I see it. If you really put yourself in your work, exercise total concentration, effort and energy, several things will happen. First, you'll learn faster and get better at what you're doing. Second, as you confront tough challenges, you'll draw more fully on your intellectual and personal resources and develop them. Third, you'll succeed and success brings rewards; personal as well as material. Both mastering a skill and making money from it are sources of inner gratification and self esteem.

To excel in any vocation, you must push yourself even when it hurts. In selling, as you know, perseverance pays off. But even the strong get weary. We've all heard about capable managers who've failed because they lacked the stamina to work under pressure or rebound from a setback. When fatigue hits and you feel headed for a burnout, here's what you might do to put yourself together.

First, try your favorite physical activity — swimming, golfing, running — it will help you relax. *Second,* keep your sense of humor. Joking about a difficult situation often puts it in a workable perspective and sometimes reduces stress. *Third,* recognize that you're human, that you will make mistakes, but they can be fixed. Recognizing your limitations is helpful because it exposes areas that need more effort on your part. But in the end, like that British runner, a manager's ability to stay on course comes only from tenacious self-discipline. The French scientist Louis Pasteur said: "Let me tell you the secret that led me to my goal. My strength lies solely in my tenacity."

In the current business climate, you must persevere to survive. I know that stimulating a sales force today is a demanding task. You must be able to inspire yourself as well as others and encourage those under you to carry on when they get weak.

It's a tall order — because they're buffeted by a negative environment all day. The economy, the dealers, the customers who keep saying: "No, never mind, not this time, check with me next month." Your sales reps can come back in bad shape. Down, disappointed, sometimes depressed, they look to you for support and guidance.

You must be understanding and yet make demands, insist on productivity, in spite of the desolation in the marketplace. Sometimes, a manager must sound an optimistic note against a chorus of pessimists, which is a subtle but indispensable management skill. Most of all — you must inspire your people to inspire themselves.

The word "manage" derives from the Italian "mano" for hand and management connotes a skillful handling of people. Textbooks contain many useful ideas, but they can't teach you to inspire those working for you. When you get down on a one-to-one basis, an individual's instinct beats academic precept every time. Your approach may vary from friendly persuasion to the iron hand in velvet glove, to no gloves at all. The aim is to make them feel that their work is important and that achievement can bring fulfillment.

The ability to manage people under stressful situations requires a delicate balance of firmness and compassion. You must offer constructive criticism together with words of praise. A wise man once said: "Praise, of all things, is the most powerful excitement to commendable actions, and animates us all in our enterprise. "More mature individuals are instinctively able to strike this balance. Others cultivate it, over time, through self-scrutiny and a genuine interest in people. And there are those who never develop it. They become frustrated and angry with the human side of managing.

Yet cultivating this interpersonal side doesn't mean you stop demanding results. That's another skill which involves psychological savvy. In fact, the capacity for making demands and getting people to meet them is among the most underdeveloped managerial talents.

Why? Making demands might appear risky. You might imagine they'll provoke resistance from subordinates and result in embarrassment for not reaching them. A manager might also rationalize by saying he's already done everything possible in establishing expectations. That's a strategy for self-defeat.

On the other hand, if you're convinced that you want

better results and are willing to put in the time and energy, you can get them. First, you have to figure out your objectives. In establishing them, it's wise to sound out your subordinates on opportunities for improvement. Their responses will provide clues about their readiness. But remember, sounding them out doesn't mean giving up concrete performance expectations. The next important step is to communicate precisely what you expect. It's crucial to make it absolutely clear that you're not asking permission to set goals or seeking advice on whether they're attainable, but saying unequivocally that they must be achieved.

Now, I know from experience, that when a manager tells subordinates that better results are in order, they might, at first, not take him seriously, or even resort to testing him. They might imply that his expectations are unrealistic. Such testing is sometimes an expression of their anxiety about meeting demands and a way of seeking reassurance from the boss. This situation presents a real chance to show leadership and inspire people.

If you have confidence in yourself, you'll be able to accept the testing, help subordinates deal with any feelings of incompetence, all this — without lowering your expectations for productivity. If you can "hang tough" on demands while truly helping people meet them, you'll no doubt find that many anticipated difficulties failed to materialize.

Instead, your subordinates will respond to more rigorous demands, become more productive, and take pride working in a results-oriented environment that you've created by fully exercising managerial authority.

Pollster Daniel Yankelovich says most Americans still believe in working hard because of an inner need to perform. He suggests that management emphasize the "soft" factors of production, like job dedication and implies that capital investment isn't the only way to high productivity.

This brings me back to my main idea: if you can inspire dedication, you have a better chance of increasing productivity. So far I've said that people are inspired by believing in themselves and emulating others. I observed that the role of a manager is to be understanding and supportive to his or her staff especially during tough economic times. It's often difficult to show genuine concern

for your staff, without over-identifying with them and com-
promising the authority necessary for leadership. You
must judge when it's OK to go for a drink with your staff
after work. You should be able to discuss someone's family problems if you sense it might improve their job
performance.

Cultivating these skills does not relieve you of the obli-
gation to provide practical mundane assistance to your
sales staff. If someone is having trouble with any aspect
of the job, you must meet them more than halfway. If
people have a chance to talk about problems in a candid
and non-threatening context, solutions might be found.

You might think it's easier to fire somebody and comfort
yourself saying: "I'm sorry you just don't have the stuff to
be a sales rep." If you say that after making every effort
within your power to help an individual, you're home free.
But, if you didn't give that person all you can, you've done
an injustice and failed to carry out your supervisory responsibility. Think twice before you dismiss somebody
and ask: "Did I do enough?"

I feel that the "exit" interview reveals much about the
quality of management. In a situation where someone is
leaving by choice, only one question need be asked.
"Would you come back to the company?" Or put another
way, "Would you recommend that a family member or
friend work here?" A company, like an individual, gets its
reputation from its dealings with people. And if it does not
do well by them, some will just quit. Others who can't will
stay on becoming uninspired, cynical and unproductive
employees. A recent book put forth the theory of a unique
corporate "culture," but this notion was already known to
Shepard who, in his *Laws of Economics* wrote: "Behind
each corporation must be the singular force, or motive,
that sets it apart from any other corporate structure and
gives it its particular identity."

People indicate their feelings about an organization by
deed as well as word. If they feel positive about it,
chances are they'll be more productive. So you can see
that management through inspiration can have an impact
on the bottom line. Each of you will succeed to the extent
that you inspire yourself and those around you.

In this business, you must at times make tough decisions that could result in hardship to someone on your
staff. Being hardnosed about productivity and profits

never justifies undignified behavior toward anyone. That's something I learned from Saul Yaffa who was a compassionate person and competent manager. In this tradition, I would like to leave feeling that people thought of me as someone in whom they could confide, as one who could criticize their work if need be, and as one who was open to suggestions. I'd also like to be seen as one who made decisions and implemented them firmly and fairly.

I guess every man likes to pass on something of value to those with whom he's shared an important part of his life. This isn't meant to be my secret for success, but a few simple reminders:

First — Define yourself by what you do, by how you treat others, and how they see you.

Second — Define your business goals clearly so that others can see them as you do.

Third — Praise good work loudly and criticize shortcomings softly.

Fourth — Follow your instincts, those undefinable feelings that can warn you of dangerous ventures or help you bring out the best in people.

Finally — Put all you have into each working day and you'll find the deep fulfillment you desire.

This is my legacy offered humbly with high regard for your work and sincere appreciation for your friendship. Thank You.

All speeches reprinted by permission of "Vital Speeches of the Day."

Endnotes

1 ''Graphic Reinforcement for an Oral Presentation'' by Lee
Pitre and Larry Smeltzer in the *ABCA Bulletin*.
2 *The Person in Psychology* by Gordon Allport.

Other Communication
Skills for Career Success

HOW TO GET A JOB — INTERVIEWING STRATEGIES

How often do you think of your present role as a student as an investment in your future? If you don't (think of education as an investment) you should, and if you do, you're on the right track. What you are doing now as a student may be the best investment you will ever make and, like all sound investments, you can expect to receive future dividends. The extent of those dividends was made very clear in a recent study which indicated that men and women who graduate from college earn substantially more money in their lifetimes than those who do not graduate. (An additional $340,000 for men; $190,000 for women.) In fact, there is a higher lifetime increment of earnings for every additional year that you remain in school.

The above statistics are good news and should reassure you that the time, effort, and money that you are investing now are well worth the effort. However, in order to reap the dividends that you have earned, you must first be successful in obtaining employment. The difficulty of finding a job will vary with the state of the economy, career preferences, and other personal factors, but it is rarely, if ever, easy. Finding a job you will be happy with is a task that must be approached in a systematic and organized way in order to achieve your objective. Take this opportunity to learn how to go about obtaining employment. After all, wouldn't it be foolish to have worked hard on your investment and not be able to take the last step which allows you to collect your earned dividends?

An orderly way to begin is to think of your job-search as a process which occurs in three stages. The three stages are: *1/ Pre-Interview Activities, 2/ The Interview, 3/ Post-Interview Activities.*

Pre-Interview
Activities

Most of the conventional wisdom on preparing for an interview begins with tips about researching potential employers or writing resumés or application letters. We will make those suggestions also, but a 1984 report on employment prospects compiled by Placement Director Victor Lindquist and his predecessor, Frank Endicott, at Northwestern University offers other advice. The report, based on a survey of 262 corporations, states that recruiters look for college graduates with summer or part-time work experience, preferably in a related or usable field. According to the report, students who do not work while in college and do not plan for the future will have more difficulty finding a job. One recruiter was quoted as saying, "The attitude that I should enjoy my college years and worry about employment later is totally unrealistic." Another suggested that students learn how to speak, write, and get along with people. In other words, the message is to develop your communication skills and to start *now* to prepare for the future, not immediately before or after graduation.

Locating
Employers

The most logical place to start searching for a prospective employer is with your college or school's Placement Office, if one is available. They attract companies to campuses for the purpose of hiring students like yourselves. Part of the fees that you pay support this Placement Office so you are mistaken not to use its services.

In addition to attracting potential employers, Placement Offices often offer information on resumés, application letters, and interviewing techniques. Even if you do not get hired through your Placement Office, you can gain valuable interviewing experience which will help in subsequent interviews. Indeed, many Placement officers will recommend that students sign up for interviews if only for the practice. Evidently, they agree with Jeffrey Allen, the author of *How to Turn an Interview Into a Job,* who states that interviewing is like tennis in that both depend upon approach, practice, and hundreds of conditioned responses.[1] More on that later.

If you do not have access to a Placement Office, you must turn to sources which are available in the reference sections of local libraries. Librarians will help you find books which list names, addresses, and telephone numbers of companies by industry. In addition, you may read the corporate profiles which appear in *Dun and Bradstreet's Million Dollar Directory, Standard and Poor's Register of Corporations, Directors and Executives,* and *MacRoe's Blue Book.* Your state publishes indexes to manufacturers, service firms, and retail firms as well as a census of businesses. Perhaps the most readily available source of corporate information is the Phone Book *Yellow Pages.* These are just some of the obvious sources to use at the start of your search. There are many more should you need them.

Once you have focused on certain companies, you need to learn all that you can about those companies. This is done by obtaining annual reports, reading industry trade magazines, or, when possible, talking to people who work for those companies. Find out what the present financial status of the company is, what are its future plans, what is its operating "philosophy", how do its employees feel about working there, and what products or services are its business. You need to have this knowledge so that should an interviewer pose the much-asked question, "Tell me what you know about our company and why you want to work here," you will be able to give a knowledgeable reply and not draw an embarrassed blank.

Writing the Resumé and Letter of Application

Once you have targeted some prospective employers, you now have to begin packaging the product you are selling which, of course, is yourself. Specifically, you need to write a resumé and a letter of application.

The resumé and letter of application have only one purpose and that is to get you a personal interview. Together, the two pieces are a kind of advertising piece which, like any advertising, must be persuasive. They must arouse the employer's interest, build a case which distinguishes you from other applicants, and motivate the employer to grant you an interview. As such, the resumé and letter of application must be brief, easily read, contain all relevant information, and present you in your most positive light. Here is a sample resumé in a format that is appropriate for the student about to venture into the job market.

Sample Resumé

Robert Dalton
12 Caswell Street
Holden, MA 27510

PROFESSIONAL OBJECTIVES:

To obtain a position as Sales Management Trainee — leading
to a position of increased responsibility.

EDUCATION:

9/80 to 6/84 — Providence College; B.S. Business Management Cum Laude

9/76 to 6/80 — Holden High School

KEY SUBJECTS STUDIED:

Principles of Marketing, Management Seminar, Public Relations, Psychology, Business Writing, Communication Skills

WORK EXPERIENCE:

6/81 - 9/81 — Holden Country Club — started as golf caddy;
6/82 - 9/82   advanced to caddy supervisor; also assisted in
6/83 - 9/83   sales and merchandising in the Pro Shop.

EXTRACURRICULAR ACTIVITIES:

Yearbook Sales Manager — 3, 4; Varsity Baseball — 1, 2, 3,
4; Marketing Club — 1, 2, 3, 4

Also enjoy skiing, tennis, jogging, and playing the piano.

REFERENCES:

Available upon request.

Note that the above sample resumé presents an abbreviated
biography which summarizes and highlights the applicant's
education, work experience, and distinctive achievement.
Should you be applying for jobs that require different skills,
you might want to change the emphasis of a section to better
suit the situation.

Resumés are always accompanied by a letter of application
which is intended to reinforce, but not duplicate, the informa-

tion on the resumé. The letter should be brief (one typed page), and it should be mailed to the individual who makes employment decisions. You can write an effective letter of application if you follow these suggested steps:

- State the purpose of the letter (that you wish to be considered for employment).

- Explain what accomplishments and/or skills you have which the employer will benefit from should they hire you.

- Ask for the opportunity to present yourself in person during a personal interview. This is an all-important point that enables you to keep control of your job search. (See last section of letter that follows.)

Sample Cover Letter

12 Caswell Street
Holden, MA 27510
June 8, 1984

Mr. Theodore Banks
Marketing Manager
Cross Manufacturing Incorporated
14 River Street
Boston, MA 64712

Dear Mr. Banks:

As a recent graduate in Business Management from Providence College, I feel I am qualified and would like to apply for the position of Sales Management Trainee with Cross Manufacturing.

As you can see by my resume, my time at Providence College was active and successful. Specifically, I believe I have acquired the understanding of people and the communication skills needed to be a dynamic and productive sales manager.

Further, the practical experience I gained during my three summers at the Holden Country Club should serve me well. Not only were those summers a valuable learning experience, but I now know that I am capable of and enjoy supervising others and selling products.

I would like to have an interview with you and will call you on Tuesday morning, June 25th for that purpose. I hope to be able to meet with you soon. Thank you.

Sincerely,

Robert Dalton

If you follow up your letters of application and resumes as suggested, you will soon have appointments for interviews. Prior to those interviews, your preparation should include reading as much about the companies as possible and determining and practicing your responses to the questions that you know you are certain to be asked.

**Following-Up
Letter of
Application**

For some time, it has been common knowledge that you should not try to call people to schedule interviews on Mondays or on Friday afternoons. Instead, place your calls Tuesday through Friday between 9:00 a.m. and 11:00 a.m. Your chances of talking to the person you wish to reach and getting the desired response will be increased this way.[2]

Think of your phone call as a logical extension of the statement you made at the end of your letter of application, that you would be calling for an appointment. Refer back to your letter by giving the date it was written and its purpose. You will get one of three responses: 1/ be told you will not be granted an interview 2/ be told to contact the company at a later date for an interview 3/ or be given an interview. All three are desirable responses, even the first one. If a company has no genuine interest in you as a prospective employee, then you need to know that fact so that you do not waste time, energy, or hope pursuing a dead end. Determine your own fate; find out what you need to know.

If possible, try to schedule two interviews a day. Consider this your job until a paying one comes along. Work hard at it, and you will improve your interviewing techniques.

The Interview

Employment interviews are stressful experiences which can cause nervousness and anxiety which, if not controlled, can interfere with your ability to do your best during an interview. Knowing this, you need to try to minimize the effects of stress. Get a good night's sleep and exercise regularly when you are job-hunting. Feeling healthy and knowing that you look your best can boost your confidence and help to offset stress.

Dress appropriately. For men the most appropriate dress is a navy blue three-piece suit, white dress shirt, dark striped tie, and black dress shoes. Women have more flexibility but a conservative dress or suit in subdued colors is best. Be on time and, when you are ushered in to meet the interviewer, smile warmly, look the interviewer in the eye, and firmly shake his or her hand. Show your enthusiasm, use positive language, express a reasonable confidence in your own abilities, and sell yourself. Relax and enjoy the occasion. Remember that the interviewer is just a person carrying out his job and, just as with you, he or she has certain objectives which you need to know.

The Interviewer

Corporate interviewers generally share the same objectives. They want to hire qualified applicants who will perform their jobs well and who will remain with their new employer for a reasonable period of time. To do this, interviewers employ different techniques. In addition to the customary one-on-one interview, some companies require multiple interviews and the actual hiring decision is made by a group or committee. Others engage in "stress" interviews while some companies ask the job candidate to participate in social occasions such as lunches, dinners, or other functions. Whatever the interviewing method, similar patterns emerge. Interviewers ask questions and interviewees give responses. Through this process the interviewer hopes to learn enough about you to help him/her make a decision. True, there is also the opportunity for you to pose questions about the company, but these are less significant to the evaluation process unless you blunder and ask naive questions about vacation time or unrealistic pay levels.

Because this question-answer format is so standard, you can prepare for it by anticipating the questions that will be asked and how to respond to them. Understand that the "real" reason for a question might not be the same as the actual wording of the question itself but in what your answer might reveal about the type of person you are. Study the questions that follow, write answers that are consistent with the person you want to be, and rehearse them. Your goal is not to respond with memorized, canned replies but rather to be able to respond confidently knowing that you have already considered the questions and are comfortable answering them.

Common Interview Questions

1/ Tell me about the college you attended. Did you enjoy it?

2/ What were your favorite courses? Why?

3/ Did you do the best work you were capable of in college?

4/ What are your career objectives?

5/ Do you work well with others?

6/ What is your major strength or talent?

7/ What is your major weakness?

8/ Do you like to travel?

9/ Are you willing to move if the job requires it?

10/ Do you read as a leisure time activity? Who is your favorite author?

11/ Would you describe yourself as a heavy television viewer? What programs do you like?

12/ What kind of personality do you have?

13/ Do you consider yourself creative?

14/ Are you active in any athletic activities?

15/ How much money would you like to be making in ten years?

16/ Do you take criticism well?

17/ Tell me about yourself.

18/ For what type of supervisor would you prefer working?

19/ Why do you want to work for our company?

20/ Why should we hire you?

You will be asked some of the above questions or variations of these questions. Count on it. Also, if you are applying for a job in a specific job category, you can expect questions designed to test your knowledge of specific job skills. Be sincere in your replies, but do try and present yourself in the best light. Here are some possible answers to a few of the more difficult questions:

Interviewer: What is your major weakness? *(Question 7)*

Reply: Sometimes I stretch myself too thin by trying to do too many things at once. I need to learn to manage my time and my priorities better.

Interviewer: How much money would you like to be making in ten years? *(Question 15)*

Reply: I don't know that I can set an exact dollar figure. However, I would like to feel, if I make contributions of value to the company, that I would be rewarded fairly so that I could take care of my responsibilities to my family.

Interviewer: For what type of supervisor would you prefer working? *(Question 18)*

Reply: It doesn't matter to me if it is a man or woman as long as that person is fair, can provide the guidance I will need, and will recognize that I have performed my job well.

Interviewer: Why should we hire you? *(Question 20)*
Reply: You should hire me because I will be an asset to your firm. I am bright, have lots of energy, and I am willing to work hard to achieve goals.

The Question of Salary

If you do your pre-interview homework and prepare yourself to answer the predictable questions, the time will come when the delicate issue of salary will be raised. Here there are two extremes to avoid: *1/ don't undersell yourself,* and *2/ don't price yourself out of consideration by stating an unrealistic salary amount.* You will be more effective if you are governed by two questions:

1/ What is the general salary range for the job?

2/ What amount of money do I need to support myself?

Go into the interview with a salary goal based on the answers to these two questions and also have a lowest acceptable figure in mind.

Inquire as to how often salary reviews occur and what level of increases are given. Keep in mind that fringe benefits such as life insurance, health insurance, and pensions have a dollar value to them and are part of your overall compensation package. If a company wants to hire you, they should offer you a fair wage. If they don't, you probably don't want to work for them anyway.

Post-Interview Activities

Your interview is over. If you have been offered a job, congratulations, for you are the exception. Most worthwhile jobs are *not granted* during the first interview. Offers are made after other prospects have been interviewed and consultations have taken place. Therefore, you need to keep busy doing the following things:

- Immediately after an interview, critique your performance. What did you do well and what not so well? How can you be more effective next time? Plan to make the necessary adjustments.

- Go on to your next interview. Until you secure a job, interviewing is your job.

- Most important of all, write a follow-up note to every interviewer that you have met. Thank them for their time, restate your desire for employment and why you would be an asset, and then request a decision in a reasonable period of time. Your letter will refresh the interviewer's memory of you, impress him with your thoughtfulness and drive, and just might separate you from other prospects who do not take the time to write a follow-up letter. Here is a sample follow-up letter:

Sample Follow-Up Letter

10 Bell Street
Miami, Florida
June 15, 1984

Mr. Robert Sharpe
Personnel Manager
Carter Company
10 Main Street
Miami, Florida

Dear Mr. Sharpe:

Thank you for the time and attention you gave to me today. I enjoyed meeting you and the people in your office.

Our meeting confirmed my belief that Carter Company is a firm for whom I would be happy to work. I am hopeful that you feel my education and work experience would make me a welcome addition to your company.

I am eager to get on with my career and hope to hear good news from you within the next two weeks.

Thanks Again.

Sincerely,

Linda Anderson

Follow the suggestions made in this chapter, and put into effect the other principles of communication that you have learned, and your job hunt will be successful. *Good luck.*

*Read the *Management-Trainee Employment Interview* that follows. It provides excellent examples of typical interview questions and some very effective responses.

Management-Trainee Employment Interview

Opening

MICHAELS: Hi! (Smiles) Sharon Young?

YOUNG: Yes.

MICHAELS: (Greets applicant with a handshake) I'm Len Michaels, Personnel Director for Parker House Restaurants and I'll be interviewing you today for the Management Trainee position you applied for. Won't you have a seat?

YOUNG: Thank you.

MICHAELS: (Asks an "ice breaker" question) Did you have any problem finding the office?

YOUNG: No, not really, When I was here before to complete the application form, I asked the secretary if this was where they'd hold the interviews and she said yes. So I didn't have any problems at all.

MICHAELS: Very good. (The interviewer now makes a transition to the body of the interview) What I'd like to do this afternoon is find out something about you — your educational and work background. Then I'd like to discuss the qualifications for this job and, finally, I'd be happy to answer any questions that you may have about Parker House in general and the management-trainee position in particular.

YOUNG: Fine, I'm ready to go.

Body

MICHAELS: As a starting point, could you please tell me what you think you could offer Parker House?

YOUNG: Well, I'm a self-starter and I work well with most types of people. I pick things up very quickly and I have had specific work experience with Burger World, two summers, and two years with the Fisherman's Restaurant. The psychology, communication, accounting, and management courses that I completed in college should also help me as a manager at Parker House.

161

MICHAELS: What were some of your duties at Burger World: (Interviewer is seeking work experience information)

YOUNG: The first summer I worked the grill and the friers, took orders, and worked the register. The second summer I was shift supervisor for the afternoon/evening shift and I cashed out all the registers and made the bank deposits.

MICHAELS: And your duties at Fisherman's?

YOUNG: The first year I worked in the kitchen preparing dinners and salads. Then one of the hostesses quit and I took over her position and helped Mr. Mann with the daily deposits and the books.

MICHAELS: That sounds like a pretty varied experience. Did you encounter any problems while you were at Fisherman's?

YOUNG: I'm not sure what you mean by problems ... Do you mean personal problems or work-related problems? (The applicant asks for clarification when unsure of the question)

MICHAELS: I mean work-related problems.

YOUNG: There were times when reservations got backed up and so you had to ask customers if they would like to have a drink at the bar while they waited for their table to become available. Sometimes one of the kitchen crew wouldn't show for some reason and we'd have to pitch in and help. Things like that ... nothing serious though.

MICHAELS: You mentioned Mr. Mann, was he the owner?

YOUNG: Yes, he and his wife owned the restaurant.

MICHAELS: What did Mr. Mann do about the people who didn't show for work?

YOUNG: If they had a legitimate excuse but did not call before their shift, he gave them a warning. If it happened again — as it did once — he would fire them.

MICHAELS: I take it you've never fired anyone?

YOUNG: No, I haven't.

MICHAELS: Would you be able to terminate or fire any-one? (The interviewer is trying to discover how the applicant would handle this conflict situation)

MICHAELS: (Pause) If there were just cause, I guess I could. Does Parker House have a specific policy on this, Mr. Michaels?

MICHAELS: We can cover that later in the interview, but Sharon, what I'd like to explore with you for a moment is what your feelings would be if you had to fire someone.

YOUNG: Sure. (Pause) If someone had done something against company policy, like not showing for a shift and not calling, then the employee would warrant termination. If, for example, the person did a sloppy job of cleaning a stove ... I'd *tell* them and *show* them how it was to be done, and then I'd have them show me how it was to be done. I would explain to them that the sloppy work should not happen again. If it did, then you'd have to let them go.

MICHAELS: If a customer complained that his food was not cooked properly how would you handle it? (Again, another question which seeks to determine how the applicant would handle a conflict situation)

YOUNG: If his food were not done, I'd find out what was not cooked properly. I'd apologize and find out how the customer wanted it cooked. I'd then ask the cook to prepare it to the customer's specifications and I'd make sure to offer another apology after the dinner was returned to the customer. I'd make sure to check back later and find out if everything was satisfactory.

MICHAELS: On your resumé you list that you have a two-year degree from Lock City Community College in New York and a B.A. from Columbus College. (pause)

YOUNG: Right.

MICHAELS: What courses do you think would be helpful in managing a Parker House restaurant? (Interviewer is attempting to discover what educational experiences would be related to this position)

YOUNG: The psychology courses would be helpful in understanding customers and employees. The public speaking course helped me to gain confidence in myself and helped me to improve my communication ability. The interpersonal communication course helped me to learn how to resolve conflicts between myself and others and to work with other people. The management courses would certainly be relevant for organizing, hiring, training, and managing employees. The economics and accounting courses have given me a background for the bookkeeping and the food ordering aspects of the job.

MICHAELS: Umm, hum, I see. (Pause) Any other courses that you could think of that would be helpful?

YOUNG: I took two non-credit food preparation courses at Lock City College, one in dinner preparation and the other in dessert preparation. (Pause) When I was a freshman in high school my mother said I had something to learn about cooking.

MICHAELS: Does your mother think that you've improved?

YOUNG: Oh yes!! (Smiles) She helped me a lot, and those courses and then Fisherman's have given me a pretty good foundation.

MICHAELS: Is there anything about cooking you really dislike?

YOUNG: Nothing major, but I never did get the hang of lemon meringue pies.

MICHAELS: (Smiles and nods) I take it that you enjoy cooking?

YOUNG: Very much! I like to experiment with foods. But I also enjoy being "out front," meeting people, making them feel comfortable.

MICHAELS: How would you rate the education you received from Columbus?

YOUNG: Columbus has an excellent business management program and I am glad that my father got transferred. I was a little apprehensive about the move at first and about attending Columbus. However, the academic training and experiences I received from Columbus supported the foundation courses that I took at Lock City College.

I think the grades I earned at both colleges reflect just as much about my capabilities as they do about the schools' educational programs. The teachers, for the most part, were sensitive to student needs, were challenging and motivating, and were realistic and practical in what they taught.

I also got to learn something about myself, who I was, and what I wanted to do with my life. (pause) Probably the most important factors of college life are that it helps you to understand yourself and other people and how to get along with and work with other people.

MICHAELS: (Smiles) What about strengths and weaknesses; we all have them. What would you say is your biggest strength?

YOUNG: I like to be organized, to anticipate problems and how to solve them. And I like working with people.

MICHAELS: Why do you like to work with people? (Interviewer probes for more specific information)

YOUNG: (Pause) I can't really put my finger on it, but I worked with a lot of different people in my life. I guess I got this from home. There was always someone at the house — neighbors, friends, relatives, and so forth. In high school and college I was working with people to solve mutual problems — like on the Student Senates at Lock City College and Columbus College.

MICHAELS: What's your biggest weakness?

YOUNG: (Pause) I don't like people who are gossips. One of my best friends got hurt by gossip stories that weren't true. And I guess I get short-tempered with people who constantly slack-off; who do just enough to squeak by in doing a job.

MICHAELS: I see. Excluding age, racial background, and gender characteristics, what types of people do you like to work with most? (Notice that the interviewer is tacitly telling the applicant that he does not wish to pursue material which might be classified as unlawful according to the Civil Rights Act of 1964)

YOUNG: I like to work with people who are organized; who try to do a job right the first time rather than having to do it over again. I like to work with people who are willing to "hop" right in and help others if a problem occurs. I guess I prefer to work with people who are *willing* to work with others. It doesn't matter if they are quiet or outgoing, but, like I said, I can work with a lot of different types of people.

MICHAELS: Let me tell you about this management trainee position and what Parker House can offer *you*.

We start all of our management trainees out with a twelve-week, intensive, training orientation. This pamphlet outlines in detail (smiles and hands applicant the pamphlet) what the training sessions are all about.

Basically, you will be rotated through all of the basic operations and procedures that all of our restaurants follow: cooking, dishes, register, waitressing, hosting, record and bookkeeping, ordering, scheduling, employee evaluations, and supervision.

During these three months you are on probationary status and if you do *not* work out you can be terminated. The pay for these three months would be 265.00 per week. Room and board will be paid for by the company during this three month orientation, and the day you begin your training you'll be covered by our medical and dental insurance policies.

After the orientation program you will be assigned to a Parker House restaurant in the greater Columbus area for a period of nine months. What happens during these nine months is explained in another pamphlet. (Hands the material to the applicant and smiles)

Essentially, during these nine months you will be a shift supervisor and you will work very closely with the manager of the restaurant — sort of like the "buddy-buddy" system. The manager will reinforce what you learned in the orientation sessions. For these nine months your pay will be elevated to 300.00 per week.

After one year with the company you will be eligible for a one-week paid vacation. In the second year you *could* be offered an assistant manager position with an area restaurant with a *minimum* pay of $350.00 per week.

Finally, after the second year you could move up to manager status by bidding on a restaurant — bidding is done by seniority — and this move may involve a relocation on your part.

Well, Sharon, I guess that's the best summary I can

offer of our policy for trainees, supervisors, and managers. Is it too much to digest too quickly?

YOUNG: No, Mr. Michaels, it seems to fit together very nicely.

MICHAELS: I have a lot of information about you, Sharon. Would you have any questions that *you* might want to ask?

YOUNG: During this twelve week orientation, what type of hours would I be working?

MICHAELS: Sessions start at 8:45 a.m. You'll spend two hours in class and one hour in the kitchen. Then there's a lunch break. When you return from lunch there are another two hours of class and a one-hour demonstration. Finally, you have a one-hour classroom summary and then dinner.

Trainees usually spend a couple of hours in the evening preparing for the next day's orientation sessions. The remaining part of the evening is free time as are Saturday afternoons and Sundays.

YOUNG: So, there are classes on Sunday mornings?

MICHAELS: Classes are held from 10 until noon.

YOUNG: I see. What about shift hours for the nine months following the orientation?

MICHAELS: Sharon, the schedule would be determined by the restaurant manager. However, you would be working one of the three shifts during those nine months. Most likely you would start on the 11 p.m. to 7 a.m. shift because that would be the shift with the least amount of activity. Then you would be eased slowly into the busier shifts.

YOUNG: What about relocation, you mentioned that it was possible. Where do you have plans for expansion?

MICHAELS: Within the next two years we will be adding restaurants in the Virginia, North Carolina, and northern and southern Florida areas. We also would like to expand in western New York and eastern Ohio.

It is premature to ask, but would you have a preference for a particular area?

YOUNG: Oh, (pause) I would not mind western New York. That's where I was born and raised. Florida would be nice — the weather is nice most of the year. (Long pause) Would there be any special requirements for clothing?

MICHAELS: No, not really. The only thing we require of our management trainees, supervisors, and managers is that they dress neatly, wear business attire, and dress conservatively on the job. (Long pause; the interviewer looks at his watch) Would there be any further questions that you would have at this time?

YOUNG: (Having seen the interviewer's clue that the interview was coming to a close) No, Mr. Michaels, I think that you have answered all the questions that I had. However, I would like to reinforce what I said earlier about my qualifications for this position. (pause)

(Smiles) I think the varied experiences that I have had in the restaurant business would help me considerably. I also believe that my educational preparation and my ability to comprehend things quickly would give me a solid foundation for the management trainee position. These two factors and my ability to work well with people should make me a strong candidate. (Pauses and smiles)

Closing

MICHAELS: It's been a pleasure meeting with you today, Sharon, and discussing your qualifications for the position. As you know we haven't finished our personal interviews with all of our candidates, but I am sure that we will have made our decisions by late Monday of next week. I will be contacting you by phone on Tuesday morning and let you know our decision at that time.

In the meantime, if you have any questions, please don't hesitate to call me at the number on my business card. (Hands candidate his business card)

YOUNG: I appreciate your time, Mr. Michaels, and the opportunity to discuss my career goals with you. I'll be home on Tuesday morning to accept your call personally. Thanks again. (Candidate extends her hand and shakes the interviewer's hand)

MICHAELS: Take care, Sharon, and have a good evening.

Reprinted with permission of Paul Seland, Niagara County Community College and Scott Foresman and Company.

10

THE CORPORATION — A NEW WAY OF LIFE

I have friends, an older married couple, who each year travel abroad to a foreign country. Prior to each trip, their preparation follows much the same pattern. They read extensively about the culture of the country they are about to visit. They try to learn as much about that culture *beforehand* as they possibly can. They study the country's history, its heroes, value systems, customs, practices, and language as much as they can. In this way they guard against "culture shock" and insure that their visit will be successful. Their preparation makes good, practical sense.

In a similar way, you who are getting ready to enter the world of business need to also engage in preparation for most corporations have their own cultures, their own way of life. In a recent book, *The Rites and Rituals of Corporate Life,* Terrence E. Deal and Allan A. Kennedy point out that businesses are living organizations whose real existence is in the hearts and minds of its employees. They contend that the culture that the employees create affects practically everything from who gets promoted and what decisions are made, to how employees dress and conduct their day-to-day business.[3] If this is so, then you need to learn as much as possible about a company's culture *before* and *after* you become part of it. This holds equally true whether you are beginning your first job in business or, later, planning a switch to "greener pastures."

In short, you need to find out all you can about your company's culture. Is the company's philosophy liberal or conservative? What services and/or products do they market? What are the beliefs and values that they hold important? How much freedom and creativity do they allow their employees? Who are their "heroes" and are employees expected to imitate them? What are their customs and rituals? What standards of behavior are expected of employees? These are just some of the aspects of corporate culture that you need to examine.

Prospective employees can learn about a company's culture from a few different sources. Find out what the company says about itself in its annual reports, press releases, and advertising. Talk to employees of the company, when possible. Use the interview to learn more. Ask questions. Generally, a conscious effort in these sources will reveal much of what you need to know. Once you have been hired however, you need to learn even more about the new culture in other ways.

The best advice for a newly arrived employee is to observe quietly and listen a lot. Learn from the "natives". They have been there longer than you and generally have much to offer. A word of caution is necessary here: beware of the disgruntled employee who, instead of working to improve the things that need improving, suffers from negativism and wishes to pass his discontent on to others. Look to those with positive messages who are tapped into the lines of corporate communication. Make your own assessment of the corporate culture and decide whether you can be happy working and living in it. Don't let others do that for you.

Grapevines

Once established in your new job, it is inevitable that you will tune into the company "grapevine". Grapevines are much like cultural universals in that every company and industry seems to have one. A *Chicago Tribune* article by Sally Saville Hodge on the subject defined the grapevine as an "unofficial source of information for everyone which hums loudest at a company that is autocratically managed or in a state of turmoil."[4] In other words, communication is much more active on the grapevine when the regular lines of communication have stopped functioning.

As a new employee, you need to listen to the grapevine even though it is the least desirable way of exchanging information. Vanessa Dean Arnold of Management World claims that, "Some studies indicate the grapevine to be 80% to 85% accurate, with inaccuracies in the form of incompleteness rather than wrong information." The problem is that the missing 15% to 20% of the message might be vital to a full understanding of the message.

The advice is simple. Use good judgement when you evaluate news from the grapevine. Ask yourself who is transmitting messages and what are their motives? Be suspect of the person who always carries bad news or who is constantly critical of fellow employees or company policies. The grapevine is part of corporate culture and, like all other parts of that culture, you need to come to understand it for what it is.

11

THE LANGUAGE OF BUSINESS

As any world traveler will attest, the foremost barrier to communication is one's inability to understand the language of people from another culture. The individual who takes the time beforehand to learn the language of the new culture he is visiting has a distinct advantage over one who does not. He is immediately accepted on a different level than the person who arrives unprepared, fumbling and awkward in his efforts to understand and to make himself understood.

In a similar way, you who are preparing for careers in business are like travelers to a new land. Business is a new way of life and, as with any culture, it has its own vocabulary. You can give yourself an advantage by learning the terms that are part of business history and are used in everyday give-and-take transactions.

The list that follows is not intended to be a complete vocabulary. That will come in time as it does to all individuals who stay in a new land. Think of the terms that follow as ones that are commonly used in the way of life you are preparing to enter. If you learn them, the transition to business will be smoother with fewer awkward moments and less culture shock. You will be able to participate fully in communication immediately without feeling like a stranger from another place who does not understand what he/she reads or hears.

Antitrust Laws — A series of laws, starting with the Sherman Act of 1890, passed by the federal government to forbid attempts by business firms to develop monopolies or restrain trade (that is, to eliminate competition through mergers and other kinds of combinations).

Aptitude Tests — Used to determine a person's probability for success in a selected job.

Arbitration — Outside neutral parties assist in resolving conflict between labor and management or their disputing parties. The arbitrator is given the authority to act as a judge in making a fair decision. If both disputing parties agree beforehand to accept the arbitrator's decision the arbitration is considered "binding".

Balance Sheet — The accounting statement that summarizes the relationship of assets (the left side of the balance sheet), on the one hand, and the claims against those assets by creditors or owners (the right side of the balance sheet), on the other.

Bear Market — A market for securities in which prices are falling and buyers are not strongly interested in buying.

Board of Directors — A group of individuals given the power by law and by vote of stockholders to manage a corporation.

Board of Governors — The governing body of the Federal Reserve System, with seven members appointed by the president of the United States to serve single, 14-year terms.

Bull Market — A market for securities in which prices are rising and buyers are interested in purchasing securities.

Capital — Buildings, machinery, tools, equipment, materials, and money that a business must have to operate; sometimes used to describe the amount of ownership in a business.

Centralized — The type of situation in which decision-making authority is concentrated at the upper levels of the organization.

Chain of Command — Means by which authority flows from top to bottom in the organization.

Collective Bargaining — The process of negotiating a labor agreement between management and labor representatives.

Computer Hardware — The machinery of computers.

Computer Languages — A collection of numbers or computer words that the computer is able to understand. Different languages may be required for different purposes.

Computer Software — Ideas, systems, programs, and methods required to run computer machinery or hardware.

Corporation — An artificial being, or person, endowed by law with most of the rights, powers, and obligations of natural persons — among them the rights to own property, incur debts, and be sued for damages.

Delegation — The process of making specific work assignments to individuals within the organization and providing them with the right or power to perform these functions.

Depreciation — The reduction of assets of a business due to wear or obsolescence.

Dow Jones Stock Averages — An index of stock prices published since 1884 and comprising 65 leading stocks, of which 30 are industrial stocks, 20 are transportation company stocks, and 15 are public utility stocks.

Entrepreneur — A person who undertakes to start and conduct an enterprise or business.

Equity — The value remaining in business or property in excess of any liability or mortgage.

Federal Reserve System — Legislation passed in 1913 established a system of 12 district Federal Reserve banks, privately owned, whose operations are under the control of the Federal Reserve Board. The principal function of the district Federal Reserve banks is to make loans to commercial banks that are members of the system. The district banks also influence the money supply by the purchase and sale of government bonds.

Grapevine — The informal means by which information is transmitted in an organization.

Income Statement — A financial statement summarizing sales for a period of time and subtracting expenses incurred in the same period to arrive at a profit or loss for the period; often called a profit and loss statement or a statement of income.

Inventory — A list of all finished goods in stock, goods in the process of manufacture, and the raw materials used, made annually by a business concern.

Job Description — Summarizes the purpose, principal duties and responsibilities of a job.

Labor Agreement — A contract between management and a union specifying terms and conditions of employment.

Line of Credit — An arrangement made by a company or an individual with a bank, giving the company or individual the right to borrow funds as needed up to a certain amount.

List Price — The price printed on the package or on a price list.

Management — The process of planning, organizing, influencing, and controlling to accomplish organizational goals through the coordinated use of human and material resources.

Management by Objectives — A systematic and organized approach that allows management to attain maximum results from available resources by focusing on specific, individual goals.

Merit-Rating System — A system for evaluating employees for possible promotion or salary increases on the basis of their performance, productivity, or merit.

Nepotism — The practice of hiring one's own relatives.

Net Worth — The claims of owners against property after the claims of all kinds of creditors have been deducted.

Partnership — A form of business ownership in which two or more persons own the business.

Policies — A predetermined, general course or guide established to provide direction in decision-making.

Prime Rate — The interest rate commercial banks charge to their best customers with an unquestioned credit rating; usually the lowest rate charged by such banks for short-term business loans.

Product Life Cycle — The idea that products are introduced, grow in sales and profitability, reach maturity, and then decline in sales and profitability.

Proprietorship — A business owned and controlled by one person. Also, in accounting, the claims of owners against property after claims of all kinds or creditors have been met. Also called capital or net worth.

Quality Circles — Groups of people working together who meet regularly to discuss work-related problems and solutions.

Small Business Administration (SBA) — The federal agency that provides financial, managerial, and procurement assistance to small businesses.

Span of Management — There is a limit to the number of employees a manager can effectively supervise.

Specialization — Employees concentrate their efforts on one particular activity or subject.

Strategic Planning — The determination of how the organizational objectives will be achieved. Primarily accomplished by top-level management.

Team Building — A conscious effort to develop effective work groups throughout the organization.

Theory X — Traditional philosophy of human nature. Suggests that motivation of employees requires managers to coerce, control, or threaten employees in order to achieve maximum results.

Theory Y — A theory of human nature that provides an alternative to Theory X. Theory Y suggests that people are capable of being responsible and mature and should be treated accordingly. Theory Y management often allows employees to participate in decision-making.

Top Management — Referred to by such titles as president, chief executive officer, vice-president, or executive director. Responsible for providing the overall direction of the firm.

Usury Laws — Laws limiting the amount of interest a lender may charge a borrower for money.

Zero Base Budgeting — Requires management to take a fresh look at all programs and activities each year rather than merely building on last year's budget.

12

THE BUSINESS MEETING — SMALL GROUP COMMUNICATION

A major part of business communication takes place in meetings where you must interact with others in small groups. The authors of *Corporate Cultures,* Terrence E. Deal and Allan A. Kennedy, contend that the most important management ritual continues to be the formal meeting. They claim all companies have them, but their form varies widely in terms of the number held, the sitting, table shape, who sits where, number and composition of attendees, and the actual conduct of the meeting.[5] Dorothy Saroff, author of *Make the Most of Your Best,* quotes a study of managerial work time done by Professor Henry Mintzberg of McGill University which shows that executives spend an average of 69 percent of their work life in meetings of one sort or another.[6] She also quotes a 1979 survey in which executives rank meetings as the fourth biggest time-waster — the first three were time on the telephone, drop-in visitors, and ineffective delegation.[7] Because of the time devoted to meetings and the potential for them to be wasteful, you need to study the nature of meetings both from the point of view of one who conducts meetings and one who is a participant.

If you are a chairperson of, or simply conducting a meeting, the best way to insure productive interchange is to prepare an agenda and send copies of it to all the participants prior to the meeting. This not only puts people on notice as to what will be discussed, but gives them the opportunity to formulate their ideas ahead of time. If you are in charge, start the meeting on time and tell the group how long the meeting will be and how much time is allotted to each topic. Encourage contributions from all present but keep the discussion on the topics listed on the agenda. *The biggest single obstacle to the successful conduct of a meeting is the tendency of speakers to wander off the topic to discuss irrelevant topics.* Everyone who has ever participated in meetings knows that. It is the responsibility of the person in charge to keep to the agenda and to courteously cut off long-winded speakers so that everyone can have their say. End the meeting on time by summarizing what was said and what actions will result from the meeting. Finally, it is good to arrange for all participants to receive a copy of the minutes of the meeting and to notify them of future meetings.

New employees normally attend meetings rather than conduct them. If this is to be your first role, follow these suggestions. When you receive an agenda, prepare your thoughts in advance; jot down notes which will serve as a reminder during the meeting. Don't be bashful. Say what you have to say, but be brief and stick to the point. Listen carefully to what others have to say, and keep your emotions under control. If all the participants conduct themselves accordingly, the sharing of ideas in group meetings can be a productive process from which both individuals and organizations can benefit.

Small Group Communication Exercises

1/ Divide class into small groups of 3 to 5 students each. Each group is to solve the same problems that are listed below. When there is *unanimous* agreement in a group on a correct answer, a spokesperson for the group may submit a written answer to the instructor.

Apply the principles that you have learned. Participate but don't dominate. Listen well. Watch for nonverbal clues. Try to improve with each problem. Repeat your strengths and change your weaknesses.

Problem A:

A man bought a horse for $50. He sold the same horse to someone else for $60. Some time later he bought back the same horse for $70. Later still he sold the same horse for $80. How much did the man make, if any, on the deal.

Problem B:

A man once looked in his wallet and noticed that he had 6 bills which totaled $63. None of these were $1 bills. Can you figure out the denomination of the 6 bills?

Problem C:

A snail starts at the bottom of a well 16 feet deep and crawls up 4 feet a day. Each night, however, the poor snail slips back 3 feet. How many days will it take the snail to get out of the well.

*Your instructor will provide you with the answers.

13 ▮▮▮▮▮

TEN TIPS ON TELEPHONE TECHNIQUES

According to John Naisbitt in *Megatrends,* the world will have one billion telephones by the end of this decade, all of them interconnected and almost all capable of dialing direct to any other.[8] Couple these statistics with the facts that the average expense of an industrial *in-person* sales call has risen to $204 per call plus every business letter costs more than $10, and you can come to your own logical conclusion. More business will be conducted by telephone in the future because it will be less expensive and it possesses the other advantage of what Naisbitt calls "instantaneously shared information." In addition, the lack of the face-to-face contact of the telephone will soon be remedied by telecommunication technology allowing conference calls, sales meetings, and sales calls by phone to take on a visual dimension. You can learn to use the telephone if you follow these tips.

- Use the telephone when subjects require immediate attention and when the subjects lend themselves to a brief phone discussion. Leave more detailed issues which do not have the same urgency to their more appropriate forum, written correspondence or face-to-face meetings.

- As part of the overall organization of your work day, plan to make most of your phone calls at the same time. Research indicates that the majority of business phone calls are not completed on the first attempt. You can increase your chances of completing your calls by calling in the mornings from Tuesday to Friday. Do not place your calls on Monday mornings or near the end of a work day unless absolutely needed.

- Before you place an important call, jot down the items you wish to discuss in the order you wish to talk about them. This habit eliminates memory lapses and the need for further calls which are more expensive and may be embarrassing or irritating.

- Identify yourself and the person whom you are calling immediately. It is the professional way. "Hello, this is George Patterson from Manville Steel. May I speak with Ruth Page?"

- Inquire about the timing of your call and then get to the point. "Ruth, do you have a few minutes to discuss the content of the training session you proposed last week?"

- Be a good listener. Apply all of the principles of active listening discussed earlier in this text. If necessary, take notes during the conversation.

- Be brief and initiate the end of the call before the other party does it. You have no way of knowing how busy the other person is and how much of an interruption your call has made. Be considerate. It will be appreciated.

- When you are taking phone messages for others, write down all the facts and put a date and time of day on the note before you deliver it.

- Be courteous to all callers and return their calls at a time convenient to you. If a person persists in not returning your calls, write a business letter containing the message and keep a copy for your files.

- Regulate the use of the phone so that it does not interfere with your work schedule. Use it efficiently for the situations which it is best suited and it will serve you well during your career.

Endnotes

1 *How to Turn an Interview Into a Job* by Jeffery G. Allen.

2 *How to Turn an Interview Into a Job* by Jeffery G. Allen.

3 *Corporate Cultures: The Rites and Rituals of Corporate Life* by Terrence E. Deal and Allan A. Kennedy.

4 "Tune into the Grapevine" by Sally Saville Hodge.

5 *Corporate Cultures: The Rites and Rituals of Corporate Life* by Terrence E. Deal and Allan A. Kennedy.

6 *Make the Most of Your Best* by Dorothy Sarnoff.

7 *Make the Most of Your Best* by Dorothy Sarnoff.

8 *Megatrends* by John Naisbitt.

Written Communication for Business

14 ||||||||

WRITTEN COMMUNICATION FOR BUSINESS

The last weapon that you need to master and include in your communications arsenal is the ability to write effective business correspondence. Perhaps at no other earlier time has the ability to write well been such a potential asset to the person aspiring to career success. There are two reasons for this. The first reason was mentioned in an earlier chapter: we live and are employed in an informational society in which work for the majority of us means processing information. Much of this information, as we shall see, is processed and communicated in writing. The second reason is that, just as the transition to an information society was occurring, the United States was experiencing the worst decline in literacy in its history. As a result, the man or woman who writes well now has a skill that separates them from so many others presently in business for whom writing is a chore that they do poorly.

College students need to know exactly what kinds of writing will be expected of them when they enter their careers. A recent study conducted by Miami University's School of Business Administration provides that information convincingly. Almost two thousand graduates from nine different business majors were surveyed as to the actual writing they were required to do in their jobs. Results from the eight hundred thirty seven respondents (42 percent) indicated that the mean percentage of time spent writing at work is 24.9 percent. Relatively recent graduates, those with five years of work experience or less, wrote significantly more often (28.4 percent of their time at work) than graduates with more than five years on the job! Think of it: more than one of every five work days is spent writing. The study also pointed out that many respondents felt writing was very important to performing their jobs as well as to advancement in their respective organizations.

Finally, the results revealed that these graduates spent the bulk of their time writing memoranda, letters, and short reports.[1] The Miami University study is supported by other reports which agree that writing skills are vital for business success.

Should you be able to sharpen your business writing skills, you will distinguish yourself from many of your peers who have not been able to do so. There has been considerable attention given to the declining scores in the Verbal Scholastic Aptitude Tests which dropped steadily from 1963 to 1981. Our public educational system has geared up for a back-to-basics movement which stresses, among other things, the fundamentals of language. Colleges and universities have had to offer students developmental courses to bring their students' language abilities up to an acceptable level. This we have known for some time. What is less widely known is the impact these declining language skills has had on businesses themselves.

It is estimated that American business loses $1 billion a year because of "foggy" writing that wastes time, kills contracts and alienates customers.[2] No wonder business is concerned and attentive to employees who are part of the problem. This unfortunate situation creates opportunities for those who write clearly and correctly. Why? Ellen Roddick, author of *Writing That Means Business* explains that "language is an item of social snobbery, and I certainly believe that people judge each other by it — at least as much as by Italian shoes or designer handbags."[3] If you write effective memos, letters, and reports, you will be judged positively by them just as the opposite of that is most certainly true.

How the Style of Business Letters Has Changed

Your lifespans have been marked by social and cultural change that is greater and more rapid, we are told, than any other period in recorded history. This statement is no doubt true, and this change has affected all aspects of our lives, including business correspondence. You need to be aware of these changes.

No longer is business correspondence overly formal, depersonalized, and mechanical. The emphasis has switched to a less formal, personal, warm, and friendly style. The worn-out expressions of the past have given way to fresh expressions of individuality with a warm tone. The idea is no longer to impress with flowery, legalistic language wrapped in lengthy sentences but to get the job done efficiently and economically using plain language and simple sentences. To do this, you need to know exactly what you are trying to accomplish with a particular piece of correspondence and how best to accomplish that objective. One of your first considerations needs to be the physical appearance of your correspondence.

The Format of the Business Letter

Whenever you sign your name to a business correspondence, that letter, memo, or report becomes your representative. It will make an impression on the reader, either positive or negative. The immediate impression will come from the appearance of the correspondence. Knowing this, make your letter look appealing by typing it on standard-sized 8½" x 11" stationery. Be neat, be brief, and remember to use paragraphing to assist the reader. Use the rewriting stage to eliminate any errors in spelling, grammar, or punctuation. There is no faster way to make a poor impression on someone than by sending them an error-filled letter.

You may use either one of two letter forms which are widely used today, the block form (see Fig. I) or the full block (see Fig. II). Both use single-spacing with double spaces between paragraphs and elements. Neither one idents paragraphs except for emphasis. The difference between the two forms is that the full block starts most elements at the left margin, including heading, complimentary close, and signature; the more traditional block form brings heading and date line, close, and signature near to the right-hand margin. Both forms are equally acceptable.

In keeping with the movement to a personal, friendly style, the trend is to personalize your salutations — to address even a stranger by name. Also, you are more consistent with a modern style when you use the warmer ''Sincerely'' or ''Sincerely yours'' rather than the more formal closings used in the past, ''Very truly yours,'' or ''Respectfully yours.''

Figure I is an unsolicited letter of application which would accompany a personal resumé. The letter shows the seven standard letter parts:

A. *Heading*
B. *Address*
C. *Salutation*
D. *Body*
E. *Complimentary close*
F. *Signature lines*
G. *Reference initials*

FIGURE I (Block)

12 Castle Road
Saunderstown, RI 02874   *A*
May 26, 1983

Mr. Thomas Benedict
Sales Manager
Canyon Department Stores   *B*
10 Main Street
Darien, CT 06820

Dear Mr. Benedict: *C*

As a graduating senior at Johnson & Wales College, with extensive on-the-job experience in retailing, I would like to be considered as a candidate for your management training program.

As part of my preparation for my Business Administration degree, I took courses in Fashion Merchandising, Marketing, Management Seminar, and Retailing as well as general courses in Communication Skills, Psychology, Sociology, and English Composition. Also, I gained valuable experience working for two trimesters in "Gladdings", which is the College's busy and successful women's retail outlet.

D

As my resumé indicates, I have spent the past three summers working for Kramer's Department Store in Westerly, R.I. My duties have included selling in both the men's and women's departments as well as working cash registers. This experience has increased my knowledge and enthusiasm for the retailing business.

I would like to have the opportunity to meet with you so that you may further evaluate my qualifications. You may contact me or I will call your office the week of June 13, in the hope of arranging an appointment.

Sincerely,   *E*

Cathy Bemis   *F*

CB:
Enclosure   *G*

Figure II is a reply to the unsolicited letter of application (Figure I). Again, note the seven standard letter parts:

A. *Heading*	E. *Complimentary close*
B. *Address*	F. *Signature lines*
C. *Salutation*	G. *Reference initials*
D. *Body*	

FIGURE II (Full Block)

CANYON DEPARTMENT STORES
10 Main St.   *A*
Darien, CT 06820

June 3, 1983

Ms. Cathy Bemis
12 Castle Road   *B*
Saunderstown, RI 02874

Dear Ms. Bemis: *C*

Thank you for your letter expressing a desire to work for Canyon Department Stores. You can be assured that both your letter and resumé have been read carefully.

I am impressed with your performance as a college student and also with your obvious enthusiasm for retailing. Although I will be on vacation until June 21st, I would like to meet with you when I return.

Would 2:30 p.m. on Thursday, June 24th be convenient for *D* you to come to Darien? If not, please call my secretary, Miss Shaw, to arrange a more suitable time.

I look forward to talking with you. The enclosed pamphlet will tell you more about our company and its philosophy.

Sincerely yours,   *E*

Thomas Benedict   *F*
Sales Manager

TB:rs   *G*
Enclosure

The Psychology of the Business Letter

All business correspondence has a quality called "tone" which most often comes from the language chosen by the writer. Tone may be described as the mood or feeling of a piece of writing. Knowing this, make a conscious effort to give your letters a positive tone by choosing words with a positive connotation. Avoid words which bring negative responses. Some years ago, a major corporation conducted a study in order to improve the quality of its employees' correspondence. One of the interesting findings of the study was that there are words that people dislike and words that people like. You can prove this to yourself by completing the short exercise that follows. To do the exercise, simply write in the blanks the first word that comes into your mind after you read each of the given words listed.

Column A	Column B
abandoned _____	achieve_____
cheap _____	faith_____
evict_____	cheer _____
stunted _____	advance_____
failure_____	popularity _____

Now, read your responses. If you are like most people, the words in Column B will have produced responses which are more to your liking than Column A. Such is the power of language and so we should pay attention to our word choices — choose positive words, words that people like to read.

Write your letters with a "you" orientation. That is, let the reader know that you are concerned about him/her. Appeal to the reader's self-interest by telling him/her how he/she may benefit in some way and try to anticipate the reader's needs by providing full information and answering questions that he/she is likely to have.

The content of your correspondence will not always be positive. Often, you will have to say "no" or be the bearer of other bad news. Still it is possible to maintain a positive tone to soften the impact of your message. You can do this by using the "sandwich" technique. Start your letter on an upbeat note ("Thank you for being one of our loyal customers for so many years. We welcome the opportunity to serve you.") and end the letter positively. ("We will put your name on our advance mailing list so that you will be notified of our special discount sales before the general public.'') These kinds of beginnings and endings have the psychological effect of making the negative message in the middle of the letter (refusing a customer's request for credit) easier for the reader to accept.

15 |||||||||

COMMON TYPES OF CORRESPONDENCE

Business correspondence may be separated into two categories: internal and external. As the terms suggest, internal correspondence is circulated and read within a company while external correspondence reaches out to a public of readers beyond other company employees. The most frequently used internal means of communication is the *Memorandum* or *Memo*. Memos may be written to an individual, a specific group of employees, or to all company employees.

Memos differ from external correspondence in that they use a basic, standardized form which allows the writer to concentrate on the essentials of the message without being overly concerned with the public relations trimmings essential to external communications. Because the reader(s) of the memo are engaged in the same area of interest, it is often permissible to use jargon or to take other shortcuts which get to the meat of the message.

It is very common for companies to provide their employees with pre-designed forms for memos. The forms will vary with the needs of a particular company but, generally, they have certain characteristics in common. The formalities that are observed in external letters, such as salutation, complimentary close, and a typed signature line are not necessary. (See Fig. III) The memorandum is not customarily signed by the writer. However, even with the added informality of the memo, the rules of effective writing still apply.

Figure III (Memo)

TO: Ann Ryan
FROM: Tom Benedict
DATE: June 3, 1983
SUBJECT: Employment Interview

I have scheduled an interview with a Ms. Cathy Bemis, a candidate for our management training program, for Thursday, June 24th, at 2:30 p.m. Do you think you could arrange to sit in on the interview so that we may benefit from your opinion of Ms. Bemis?

I am attaching a copy of her letter of application and resumé for your information. Thank You.

Figure III(a) (Memo)

TO: Tom Benedict
FROM: Ann Ryan
DATE: June 6, 1983
SUBJECT: Employment Interview

My schedule is open June 24th, and I will be happy to sit in on the interview with Cathy Bemis. Her letter and resumé show potential.

Thanks for the invitation.

Student Exercise

Using *Figure III* and *IIIa* as models, write two memos in the space provided. Assume you are the Plant Manager of a small manufacturing company and both memos are being sent to all employees. In the first memo, you are announcing good news: management had decided to close the plant at 12:00 noon on Christmas Eve so the employees can begin enjoying the holiday early with their families. Workers will be paid for afternoon hours as a form of Christmas bonus. Be sure to extend warm holiday wishes.

In the second memo, you have a more difficult job. It seems plant workers have been abusing the ten-minute coffee breaks they get each morning and afternoon. The breaks have become for some, fifteen or twenty minutes, and this is cutting into production. Using positive language, remind the employees that breaks are meant to be ten minutes and that this rule must be followed in the future.

Memo 1

TO:

FROM:

DATE:

SUBJECT:

_____

_____

_____

_____

_____

_____

Memo 2

TO:

FROM:

DATE:

SUBJECT:

_____

_____

_____

_____

_____

_____

_____

External correspondence may include a wide variety of types of letters, but studies of the day-to-day practices of large companies suggest a few basic kinds of letters are written more frequently than any others. Accordingly, it makes good sense to learn how to write these basic letters. Remember, central to the successful writing of each of these letters is the earlier suggestion to know exactly what you are trying to accomplish and how best to accomplish that objective. This is best done by remembering that business writing, like all writing, is a three-step process. In a study of how business letters are composed, John Gould found that 66⅔% of total time is spent planning, 13% reviewing, and 20% of the time is spent producing the letter. ("Experiments in Composing Letters: Some Facts, Some Myths, Some Observations," in Lee W. Gregg and Erwin R. Steinberg, eds., *Cognitive Processes in Writing,* Hillsdale, N.J.: Erlbaun, 1980, pp. 97-172). In other words, you must prewrite, write, and rewrite.

When you write a **Letter of Request,** your objective is very clear. You are attempting to obtain something that you need from another party. You may need information, services, supplies, cooperation, support, or agreement and your letter should be constructed in such a manner as to increase the chances of your getting what you need. Experience has shown that following a pattern or "formula" in these basic letters provides a solid framework on which to build an effective letter. The pattern or steps for a Letter of Request might appear like this:

1/ *State your business (what you are requesting).*

2/ *Explain the reason for your request.*

3/ *Make it easy for your request to be answered.*

4/ *Explain how the receiver of the letter can benefit from honoring your request or (if appropriate) offer something in return.*

This "formula" should not be thought of as inflexible or rigid, nor should it be considered as stifling individual creativity. Rather, it is simply an outline of the major parts typically found in Letters of Request. Read the model letter to see how a completed Letter of Request might read, then write one of your own as directed.

Figure IV (Letter of Request)

Room 116-Alumni Hall
Notre Dame, IN 46556
February 16, 1983

Mr. Robert Baldwin
President
Baldwin Associates
1 Walsh Avenue
Burbank, IL 60459

Dear Mr. Baldwin:

As a senior majoring in Business Administration at the
University of Notre Dame, I am writing a research paper on the
personnel practices of medium-sized accounting firms. Would
you be kind enough to provide answers to the following
questions to assist in my research?

1. How many employees do you have on full-time payroll?

2. How many of these are men? Women?

3. What are your annual billings?

4. What is the starting salary range of an entry-level
    accountant?

5. What is the attrition rate (first year) of entry-level
    accountants?

I am providing a stamped, self-addressed envelope for your
use. In addition, I will send you a summary of the paper along
with all vital data.

Thank you for your help.

Sincerely,

Jeff Durand

Student Exercise

Using the formula and *Figure IV* as models, write a letter of request. Assume you are an independent insurance broker. Write the Long Living Insurance Company, 12 Butler Street, New York, NY 10038, asking them to send you full information on their policies and commission schedules. You are interested in selling their coverages to your customers.

_____

_____

_____

_____

_____

_____

_____

_____

_____

_____

_____

A much more difficult letter to write is the **Letter of Refusal.** The difficulty (or challenge) exists because your letter has to accomplish a dual objective: first, the letter must say "No", and, yet, it must do so without offending the potential client or customer. This is not an easy thing to do but it can be done. As discussed in a previous section, "The Psychology of the Business Letter," "sandwiching" your refusal between a positively worded beginning and ending tends to soften the impact of the bad news. The pattern for such a Letter of Refusal contains the following steps:

1/ Soften the blow by beginning on a positive note.

2/ Say "No" positively.

3/ Offer reasons for your refusal.

4/ Offer an alternative (should there be one).

5/ End by creating goodwill.

Here is a sample Letter of Refusal built on those steps:

Figure V (Letter of Refusal)

BALDWIN ASSOCIATES
1 Wales Avenue
Burbank, Illinois 60459

February 23, 1983

Mr. Jeff Durand
Room 116-Alumni Hall
Notre Dame, IN 46556

Dear Mr. Durand:

I was interested to learn of the research project you are doing as part of your studies at Notre Dame. It sounds interesting, and I wish you success.

Since Baldwin Associates first hung out their shingle in 1948, we have adhered to a strict policy regarding the confidentiality of our personnel policies. We feel this is the way our employees would prefer it to be. We trust you will understand the reason we are not able to provide you with the information you requested.

However, I would like to suggest that you contact both the Indiana and Illinois Association of Certified Public Accountants. They are likely to have information you need though in a slightly different form.

Again, good luck with your project.

Sincerely,

Robert Baldwin
President

Student Exercise

Using the formula and *Figure V* as models, write a letter of refusal to the letter of request you wrote after *Figure IV*.

_____

_____

_____

_____

_____

_____

_____

_____

_____

_____

_____

_____

_____

_____

_____

_____

_____

_____

_____

_____

_____

_____

_____

_____

_____

_____

_____

Another type of letter with a psychological challenge is the *Letter of Claim or Complaint.* Your objective is usually quite clear; you want to notify a person or company that some service or product that they have provided you with has not been satisfactory and you want the situation remedied quickly. The problem with this letter is maintaining a balance between your frustration and disappointment and what will best accomplish your purpose. An angry outburst or an attack of sarcasm may make you feel better, but it is unlikely that it will instantly motivate someone to help solve your problem. If anything, exactly the opposite result might be obtained. Knowing this, it is good strategy to rely on a tested pattern for this important yet difficult type of letter:

1/ Begin on a positive note.

2/ State the complaint in detail.

3/ Explain the inconvenience that you have been caused (i.e., loss of business, etc.).

4/ Suggest a fair solution to the problem and a reasonable date by which you expect the problem to be solved.

5/ Express confidence that the problem will be solved and end on a positive note.

See if you recognize the pattern by numbering each of the above steps in the margin of this sample letter.

Figure VI (Letter of Complaint)

TOWER HILL MOTOR INN
18 Bridge St.
Xenia, Ohio 45385

January 5, 1983

Mr. Harold Galliger, Manager
Alliance Appliance Inc.
99 Depot Way
Xenia, Ohio 45385

Dear Mr. Galliger:

We have been a customer at your store for twelve years, ever since we first opened our business. We have always enjoyed your prompt, cooperative service.

Recently, however, we have had reason to be dissatisfied. Specifically, we purchased a 19″ color television set on December 29th for $399.00 for use in our cocktail lounge. It has not worked properly since, the main problems being a frequent loss of color and horizontal stability. Your repairman came this week and was unable to correct the problem. As a result, we have had numerous customer complaints, particularly from the crowd who had gathered to watch the Georgia-Penn State game on New Year's night. Many left to go watch the game elsewhere.

I would like you to replace the set with one that works by the beginning of next week. Please have your service representative test it thoroughly before he leaves.

I am certain you will correct this situation as quickly as possible in order to prevent further loss of business. I hope that our business relationship can continue on mutually beneficial terms.

Sincerely,

John White
Inn Manager

Using the formula and *Figure VI* as a model, write a letter of complaint. Assume you are the owner of a woman's clothing shop. An order of blouses has arrived with the cartons opened, and blouses are missing and damaged. Write a letter to the manufacturer explaining the problem and ask to have it corrected. Make up the names of the companies and the people involved.

_____

_____

_____

_____

_____

_____

_____

_____

_____

_____

_____

_____

_____

_____

_____

_____

_____

_____

_____

_____

_____

_____

_____

_____

_____

_____

_____

Letters of Claim or Complaint require replies. If the claim or complaint is unjustified, a letter of refusal (Fig. V) is in order; however, if you or your company has made a mistake, you may have to write a **Letter of Adjustment.** At first glance, this letter seems easier because it carries good news, the resolution of a problem. A closer examination of this adjustment letter reveals that, once again, there is a dual objective to be accomplished. Not only must the adjustment be made, but the confidence of the client or customer who has been wronged needs to be rewon. These steps have been proven to be successful at accomplishing both objectives:

1/ *Admit the error and apologize.*

2/ *Explain how the problem occurred.*

3/ *Make the adjustment.*

4/ *End on a positive note by creating good will.*

All businesses and people make mistakes. When mistakes happen, it is better to admit them, apologize, explain, and assure the customer that steps have been taken to prevent a recurrence of the error. Adopting this straightforward, honest approach will bring positive results. Again, number the suggested steps in the margin as you read the sample letter.

Figure VII (Letter of Adjustment)

ALLIANCE APPLIANCES INC.
99 Depot Way
Xenia, Ohio 45385

January 6, 1983

Mr. John White
Inn Manager
Tower Hill Motor Inn
18 Bridge Street
Xenia, OH 45385

Dear Mr. White:

Please accept my personal apology for the problems you
have had with the television set that was ordered for the
cocktail lounge. I have spoken with our service representative
who has assured me the problem is with the set, and the
responsibility is ours.

A check with the manufacturer revealed that there have been
similar problems with this model, and a recall is being issued.
Accordingly, I am delivering a 21″ Zenith color set to you to
replace the malfunctioning one. It will be delivered on
Monday, January 10th.

While the replacement set has a larger screen and retails for
$100.00 more than the one you ordered, there will be no
additional charge. We hope you will accept this as a token of
our good faith and that you will continue to be one of our
valued customers in the future.

Sincerely yours,

Harold Galliger
Manager

HG:jc

Student Exercise

Using the formula and *Figure VII* as a model, write a letter of adjustment to the letter of complaint that you wrote after *Figure VI*.

_____

_____

_____

_____

_____

_____

_____

_____

_____

_____

_____

_____

_____

_____

_____

_____

_____

_____

_____

_____

_____

_____

_____

_____

_____

_____

_____

_____

_____

Writing the Report

In addition to memos and business letters, the typical college-educated employee writes an average of 2.8 reports each week. The most frequently written reports are instructions and procedures; next most frequent are status reports and personnel management and employee relation reports. Other kinds of reports mentioned in the study were original research, budget reports, grant proposals, business forecasts, minutes of meetings, descriptions of mechanisms, press releases, speeches, management briefings, technical bulletins, and equipment justifications.[4]

The message should be clear. You need to learn how to write an effective business report. To do this, it is useful to define what a business report is.

A business report is an organized piece of writing which communicates information to a reader or audience for a particular purpose. Most reports are for internal consumption (inside a company or department) but many are directed at an external audience. Reports are usually written to present information, to recommend or justify an action, or to influence a decision. Some reports, such as financial reports or production or sales reports, are most common and often issued on a regular basis. While reports will vary in many respects depending on the exact situation, they all will have some things in common. To be successful, they must follow the principles of sound writing.

1/ Words and sentences must be chosen carefully so as to increase clarity.

2/ Three-part construction and the correct use of paragraphing are essential so that your report is easy to read.

209

3/ Reports need to be planned and outlined during a Pre-writing stage, written, and then carefully revised during the Re-writing stage. It is during this stage that mechanics need to be checked to eliminate all errors in spelling, punctuation, and grammar.

4/ If your report requires a particular technique of idea development, you need to use it properly and to avoid the common errors associated with that technique.

5/ Finally, your report must be complete and contain all relevant ideas and facts and, also, your information needs to be checked for accuracy.

The models and assignments that follow will give you an opportunity to imitate a few successful reports.

Figure VIII Short Business Report (External)

INDUSTRIAL CONSULTANTS, INC.
114 Wharton Street
Cincinnati, Ohio 45242

April 19, 1983

Mr. Jon Meleken, Vice President
Meleken Machine Company
611 Pearl Street
Miami, FL 36171

Dear Mr. Meleken:

*SUBJECT: Preliminary Proposal to Improve Plant Operations

After preliminary research we are ready to propose a thorough investigation of methods that will improve your overall operation, and ultimately, your profit picture.

PERSONNEL POLICIES: We propose to study methods of hiring and training workers for the purpose of improving worker productivity and reducing worker turnover.

OFFICE PROCEDURES: We shall search for possible economies in filing, accounting, and communications procedures along with better utilization of office space.

PLANT EQUIPMENT: We suggest a complete investigation of machinery and equipment to determine efficiency in comparison with possible replacements. We believe that a number of recently introduced processes would be of benefit to you.

PLANT LAYOUT: Even superior equipment may prove inefficient if the general plant layout is inefficient. We propose a study of the whole manufacturing process to determine what kind of reorganization is advisable.

We estimate that this study with full recommendations can be completed at a cost of approximately $31,500. I will call you to discuss your response to this proposal.

Sincerely yours,

John Rossman
Account Consultant

JR:br

*Please note the subject line which is being used more frequently today to call immediate attention to the topic of the report.

Figure IX Short Business Report (Internal)

TO: Maureen King

FROM: Sharon Berg

DATE: March 16, 1983

SUBJECT: Group Health Insurance Programs

After soliciting and studying proposals from six private insurance companies, I am prepared to recommend that we retain our present Blue-Cross-Blue-Shield program and set aside the idea of a private carrier.

There are three main reasons for the recommendation:

BENEFITS: (1) Without exception, Blue Cross offers broader benefits for most frequent kinds of claims. As the cost of hospital rooms continues to spiral, we are better off with semi-private coverage rather than with the fixed dollar benefit of the private companies.

EASE OF CLAIMS PAYMENTS: (2) The unquestioned acceptability of Blue Cross and its ''direct payment'' of claims is far less troublesome than having to complete separate claim forms with private companies. Also, I have checked with other companies who have switched from Blue Cross; they report a feeling of dissatisfaction on the part of employees who are not comfortable with the new claims procedures.

COST: (3) While three of the private insurance companies submitted lower quotations than Blue Cross, I do not feel the savings would continue for more than the first year of coverage. Ultimately, you pay according to your own ''experience'' and, as you know, our claims ratio has been quite high over the past five years.

Based on these reasons, my strong conviction is that we remain with Blue Cross-Blue Shield. Should you wish to see our comparative studies with all supporting data, please call me.

Exercise

Assume you are a personnel representative for a large company. You have received a resumé and interviewed an applicant for a sales position. Write a report to the Sales Manager recommending or not recommending the applicant for employment. Discuss subjects such as the applicant's academic background, previous work experience, personality, and overall potential. The applicant may be imaginary, patterned on someone you know, or even yourself.

_____

_____

_____

_____

_____

_____

_____

_____

_____

_____

_____

_____

_____

_____

_____

_____

_____

_____

_____

Endnotes

1 "What Business School Graduates Say About Writing They Do at Work; Implications for the Business Communication Course" by Gilbert C. Storms in the *ABCA Bulletin*.

2 "Well Educated Illiterates" by Didi Moore in *Self Magazine*.

3 *Writing That Means Business* by Ellen Roddick.

4 "What We Learn from Writing on the Job" by Lester Faigley and Thomas P. Miller in *College English Magazine*.

Allen, R.R., and Ray E. McKerrow. *The Pragmatics of Public Communication.* 2nd ed. Dubuque: Kendall/Hunt Publishing Company, 1981.

Barbour, Alton and Alvin A. Goldberg. *Interpersonal Communication: Teaching Strategies and Resources.* New York: ERIC Clearinghouse on Reading and Communication Skills, 1974.

Berne, Eric, M.D. *Transactional Analysis in Psychotherapy.* New York: Ballantine Books, 1961.

Centi, Paul J. *Up with the Positive – Out with the Negative.* New Jersey: Prentice Hall, Inc., 1981.

Deal, Terrence E., and Allan A. Kennedy. *Corporate Cultures: The Rites and Rituals of Corporate Life.* Addison-Wesley Publishing Company, Inc.

Dubrin, Andrew J. *Bouncing Back.* New Jersey: Prentice-Hall, Inc., 1982.

Ehninger, Douglas, Bruce E. Gronbeck, and Alan H. Munroe. *Principles of Speech Communication.* Glenview: Scott, Foresman and Company, 1984.

Fallon, William K. *Effective Communication on the Job.* New York: AMACOM, 1973.

Farrell, Thomas J. *Developing Writing Skills.* Providence: P.A.R. Incorporated, Educational Publishers, 1983.

Gilmore, John V. *The Productive Personality.* San Francisco: Albion Publishing Company, 1974.

Harris, Thomas A., M.D. *I'm O.K. – You're O.K.* New York: Avon Books, 1969.

Hunt, Gary T., and Louis P. Cusella. "A Field Study of Listening Needs in Organizations." *Communication Education.* 32 (Oct. 1983). 393-401.

Johnson, David W. *Reaching Out: Interpersonal Effectiveness and Self-Actualization.* New Jersey: Prentice-Hall, Inc., 1972.

Knapp, Mark L. *Interpersonal Communication and Human Relationships.* Newton: Allyn and Bacon, Inc., 1984.

Linkugel, Wil A., R.R. Allen, and Richard L. Johannesen. *Contemporary American Speeches: A Sourcebook of Speech Forms and Principles.* 5th ed. Dubuque: Kendall/Hunt Publishing Company, 1982.

McGregor, Georgette F. and Joseph A. Robinson. *The Communication Matrix: Ways of Winning With Words.* New York: AMACOM, 1981.

Montgomery, Robert L. *Listening Made Easy*. New York: AMACOM, 1981.

Naisbitt, John. *Megatrends*. New York: Warner Books, Inc., 1984.

Pearson, Judy C. *Interpersonal Communication*. Dallas: Scott, Foresman and Company, 1983.

Peterson, Brent O., Noel D. White, and Eric G. Stephan. *Speakeasy: An Introduction to Public Speaking*. 2nd ed. St. Paul: West Publishing Company, 1984.

Rodman, George. *Public Speaking*. New York: Holt, Rinehart and Winston, 1978.

Sarnoff, Dorothy. *Make the Most of Your Best*. New York: Holt, Rinehart and Winston, 1983.

Smelser, Neil J. *Sociology*. Alternate Edition. New Jersey: Prentice-Hall, Inc., 1984.

Smith, Dennis R. and L. Keith Williamsom. *Interpersonal Communication: Roles, Rules, Strategies, and Games*. 2nd ed. Dubuque: Wm. C. Brown Company Publishers, 1981.

Smith, Manuel J., Ph.D. *When I Say No I Feel Guilty*. New York: The Dial Press, 1975.

Tacey, William S. *Business and Professional Speaking*. 4th ed. Dubuque: Wm. C. Brown Publishers, 1983.

Valenth, Jack. *Speak Up With Confidence: How to Prepare, Learn, and Deliver Effective Speeches*. New York: William Morrow and Company, Inc., 1982.

Weinhold, Barry K. and Lynn C. Elliott. *Transpersonal Communication*. New Jersey: Prentice-Hall, Inc., 1979.

Weisinger, Dr. Hendrie and Norman M. Lobsenz. *Nobody's Perfect*. New York: Warner Books, 1981.

Wolff, Florence I., Nadine C. Marsnik, William S. Tacey, and Ralph G. Nichols. *Perceptive Listening*. New York: Holt, Rinehart and Winston, 1983.

Notes

Notes

Notes

Notes

Notes

Notes

Notes